WJEC Eduqas
Film Studies
for A Level & AS
Revision Guide

Jenny Stewart

Published in 2020 by Illuminate Publishing Limited, an imprint of Hodder Education, an Hachette UK Company, Carmelite House, 50 Victoria Embankment, London EC4Y 0DZ

Orders: Please visit www.illuminatepublishing.com

or email sales@illuminatepublishing.com

British Library Cataloguing-in-Publication Data

A catalogue record for this book is available from the British Library

ISBN 978-1-912820-35-1

Printed by Ashford Colour Press, UK

04.22

The publisher's policy is to use papers that are natural, renewable and recyclable products made from wood grown in sustainable forests. The logging and manufacturing processes are expected to conform to the environmental regulations of the country of origin.

Consultant editor: Lisa Wardle

Editor: Geoff Tuttle

Design and layout: Nigel Harriss

Cover design: Nigel Harriss

Cover image: Juice Images / Alamy Stock Photo

Screenshot acknowledgements

Beasts of the Southern Wild, dir. Benh Zeitlin [DVD], 2012, Studiocanal [2013]
Blade Runner – the Director's Cut, dir. Ridley Scott [DVD], 1982, Warner [2006]
Bonnie & Clyde, dir. Arthur Penn [DVD], 1967, Warner [2006]
Carol, dir. Todd Haynes [DVD], 2015, Lionsgate [2016]
Casablanca, dir. Michael Curtiz [DVD], 1942, Warner Brothers [2006]
City of God, (Cidade De Deus), dir. Fernando Meirelles, co-dir. Kátia Lund [DVD], 2002, Miramax [2003]
Daisies, dir. Věra Chytilová, [DVD], 1966, Second Run [2009]
Fish Tank, dir. Andrea Arnold [DVD], 2009, Artificial Eye [2010]
Frances Ha, dir. Noah Baumbach [DVD], 2012, Metrodome Distribution [2014]
Inception, dir. Christopher Nolan [DVD], 2010, Warner Home Video [2010]
La La Land, dir. Damien Chazelle [DVD], 2016, Lions Gate, [2017]
The Lady from Shanghai, dir. Orson Welles [DVD], 1947, Sony Pictures Home Entertainment [2003]
Mustang, dir. Deniz Gamze Ergüven [DVD], 2016, Artificial Eye [2016]
No Country for Old Men, dir. Joel and Ethan Coen [DVD], 2007, Paramount Home Entertainment [2008]
Nosferatu, dir. F.W. Murnau [DVD], 1922, Masters of Cinema, Eureka [2013]
Pulp Fiction, dir. Quentin Tarantino [DVD], 1994, Lionsgate [2011]
Saute ma ville, dir. Chantal Akerman, [VIMEO] 1968
Secrets and Lies, dir. Mike Leigh [DVD], 1996, Channel 4 DVD [2015]
Shaun of the Dead, dir. Edgar Wright [DVD], 2004, Universal Pictures UK [2004]
Sightseers, dir. Ben Wheatley [DVD], 2012, Studio Canal Limited [2013]
Stories We Tell, dir. Sarah Polley [DVD], Curzon Film World [2013]
Sunrise: A Song of Two Humans, dir. F W Murnau [Blu-ray], 1927, Masters of Cinema, Eureka [2011]
Taxi Tehran, dir. Jafar Panahi [DVD], 2015, New Wave Films [2016]
The Cabinet of Dr Caligari, dir. Robert Wiene [Blu-ray], 1920, Masters of Cinema, Eureka [2014]
This is England, dir. Shane Meadows [DVD], 2006, Studiocanal [2007]
Trainspotting, dir. Danny Boyle [DVD], 1996, Channel 4 [2009]
Victoria, dir. Sebastian Schipper [DVD], 2015, Artificial Eye [2016]
Vivre sa vie, dir. Jean-Luc Godard [DVD], 1962, BFI [2015]
We Need to Talk About Kevin, dir. Lynne Ramsay [DVD], 2011, Artificial Eye [2012]
Winter's Bone, dir. Debra Granik, [DVD], 2010, Artificial Eye [2011]

Photo acknowledgements

Alamy Stock Photo
AF archive: pp21, 22, 36, 65, 85, 94, 98, 40, Allstar Picture Library: pp 34, 98; Archive PL: p127; Atlaspix: pp53, 58; CBW: p74; Chronicle: p128; ClassicStock: p128; CTK: p138; Entertainment Pictures: pp86, 87, 88; Everett Collection Inc: pp35, 36, 36, 36, 37, 78, 93, 108, 109, 117, 122, 127, 85, 86, 87, 95, 140; Granger Historical Picture Archive: pp35, 43, 128; IanDagnall Computing: p128; incamerastock: p86; Interfoto: p136; Kamyar Adl: p96; Moviestore Collection Ltd: pp73, 108, 139, 87, 100 (x3); Peter Horree: p128; Photo 12: pp61, 65, 92; Pictorial Press Ltd: pp61, 128; PictureLux / The Hollywood Archive: p125; robertharding: p101; roger tillberg: p140; Science History Images: p128 (x2); ScreenProd/Photononstop: p140; Sportsphoto: pp85, 87, 99; Stacy Walsh Rosenstock: pp108 ; United Archives GmbH: pp125 ;

Getty Images
Dick Darrell/Toronto Star: p108

Shutterstock.com
p16 Fabio Pagani, FrameStockFootages; p17 Luciana Carla Funes; p26 Dfree; p37 Tinseltown; p53 Featureflash Photo Agency; p54 Andrey Bayda; p59 Twocoms; p66 deepspac, Hung Chung Chih, Everett Historical; p111 Sergio Schnitzler

Weinstein Company: pp60, 61

Contents

How to use this revision guide

Welcome to the WJEC Eduqas Film Studies for A Level and AS Revision Study Guide

Tip: We recommend that you use a notepad or word-processor to complete the activities provided in this revision guide, as there may not be enough space in the boxes provided.

This activity-based revision study guide will help you prepare for the A Level and/or AS Level Film Studies **Component 1** and **Component 2** examinations.

All sections in green are related to the **AS qualification only**

This study guide will enable you to:

- Build your confidence
- Revise all the key terms and concepts
- Build on your existing knowledge of key areas of study
- Increase your knowledge and understanding of what is required of you in the exam
- Improve your revision skills
- Prepare to function efficiently in an examination situation
- Learn what it takes to improve your grade potential.

This guide accompanies the *WJEC Eduqas Film Studies for A Level & AS Level* textbook and uses the same Case study films and extra Case study films for each section. If you have studied different films, that's ok, as you can still apply the same criteria to your own examples.

The core and specialist areas

You are expected to apply the **core areas** to every film you have studied for the A Level and/or AS Level Film Studies examinations. We will revise the key terminology for each core area on pages 12–32, then apply it to key sequences throughout this guide.

The core areas are:

- **Film form**: cinematography, editing, mise-en-scène, sound and performance
- Meaning and response: **aesthetics** and **representations**
- **Contexts**: social, cultural, historical, technological and institutional (including production).

Most study areas have at least one **specialist area** you must also revise. We will cover these areas through activities and key sequence analysis in the relevant chapters.

The specialist areas you should revise for A Level are:

- Hollywood Comparison, 1930–1990: **Auteur**
- American Film since 2005: **Spectatorship** AND **Ideology**
- British Film since 1995: **Narrative** AND **Ideology**
- Documentary Cinema: **Critical debates: Digital technology** AND **Filmmakers' theories**
- Silent Cinema: **Critical debates: the realist and the expressive**
- Experimental Film: **Narrative** AND **Auteur**

The specialist areas you should revise for AS are:

- American Independent Film: **Spectatorship**
- British Film: **Narrative**

Each chapter for the key components is structured as follows:

- An introduction to the study area with revision activities that can be applied to any of the film options in the study area.
- Revision activities for the specialist area of study (if relevant).
- Case study films with a focus on one or two key sequences.
- Sample essays with annotations to show how the assessment objectives are met.
- 'Finish it' – an activity where you can finish an exam practice question response. The opening paragraph is completed for you to set you on the right path and encourage you to look at key sequences.

This revision guide includes the following tips and activities:

Knowledge booster

Information or activities to increase your knowledge of particular components and/or Case study films.

Grade booster

Quick tips you will find useful when preparing to answer exam questions.

Revision activity

Activities to increase your knowledge and understanding of a concept, topic or film. Sometimes there may be references to particular published books which you may find useful. We don't expect you to spend extra money on these books – you may seek them out at a library, find sections on Google books or through your school or college.

Key questions

These may take the form of either quiz-style questions to test your knowledge or longer questions that test your understanding of a film or study area. The answers to knowledge-based questions are easy to find in the textbook or online.

Revision guidance on key sequence analysis

You will be expected to refer to the films you have studied in detail in the examination, even if the question does not explicitly ask you to do so. We therefore recommend that you re-watch all the films you have studied and choose key sequences or moments to analyse.

You should apply the core and specialist areas (if relevant) to your analysis. Some general questions you can use for any of your chosen key sequences are:

- How do aspects of film form create meaning in this sequence and what impact do they have on the spectator?
- How do the different aspects of film form work together in this sequence to create the overall aesthetic of the film?
- How are gender, age and **ethnicity** represented in this sequence?
- How is this sequence reflective of the film's contexts?
- How can the specialist area (if relevant) be applied to this sequence?

Answer one question from each of Sections A, B and C.

*You are advised to spend approximately **50 minutes** on your chosen question in each of Sections A, B and C.*

Section A: Hollywood 1930-1990 (comparative study)

Compare one film from group 1 and one film from group 2.

Group 1: Classical Hollywood	Group 2: New Hollywood
• *Casablanca* (Curtiz, 1942)	• *Bonnie and Clyde* (Penn, 1967)
• *The Lady from Shanghai* (Welles, 1947)	• *One Flew Over the Cuckoo's Nest* (Forman, 1975)
• *Johnny Guitar* (Ray, 1954)	• *Apocalypse Now* (Coppola, 1979)
• *Vertigo* (Hitchcock, 1958)	• *Blade Runner* (Scott, 1982)*
• *Some Like It Hot* (Wilder, 1959)	• *Do the Right Thing* (Lee, 1989).
	*To be studied in the Director's Cut version, released 1992.

Either,

1. (a)   Compare how far your chosen films reflect the auteur signature features of their filmmakers.   [40]

Or,

    (b)   Compare how far your chosen films reflect their different production contexts.   [40]

Section B: American film since 2005 (two-film study)

Answer on one film from group 1 and one film from group 2.

Group 1: Mainstream film	Group 2: Contemporary Independent film
• *No Country for Old Men* (Coen Brothers, 2007)	• *Winter's Bone* (Granik, 2010)
• *Inception* (Nolan, 2010)	• *Frances Ha!* (Baumbach, 2012)
• *Selma* (Duvernay, 2013)	• *Beasts of the Southern Wild* (Zeitlin, 2012)
• *Carol* (Haynes, 2015)	• *Boyhood* (Linklater, 2015)
• *La La Land* (Chazelle, 2016).	• *Captain Fantastic* (Ross, 2015).

Either,

2. (a)   How far do your chosen films demonstrate a constant shift between passive and active spectatorship? Refer in detail to at least one sequence from each film.   [40]

Or,

    (b)   How far do your chosen films demonstrate the importance of visual and soundtrack cues in influencing spectator response? Refer in detail to at least one sequence from each film.   [40]

Section C: British film since 1995 (two-film study)

Answer on two of the following films.

- *Secrets and Lies* (Leigh, 1996)
- *Trainspotting* (Boyle, 1996)
- *Sweet Sixteen* (Loach, 2002)
- *Shaun of the Dead* (Wright, 2004)
- *This is England* (Meadows, 2006)
- *Moon* (Jones, 2009)
- *Fish Tank* (Arnold, 2009)
- *We need to Talk about Kevin* (Ramsay, 2011)
- *Sightseers* (Wheatley, 2012)
- *Under the Skin* (Glazer, 2013)

Either,

3. (a)   How useful has an ideological critical approach been in understanding the narrative resolution of your chosen films?   [40]

Or,

    (b)   How useful has an ideological critical approach been in understanding binary oppositions in the narratives of your chosen films?   [40]

WJEC Eduqas Specimen Assessment Materials

The Component 1 and Component 2 A Level Film Studies examinations consist of essay-style questions.

In the **Component 1** examination, you will write three essay-style answers worth 40 marks each. The total exam time is **2 hours and 30 minutes**.

This examination paper is worth 35% of your overall A Level grade.

In the **Component 2** examination, you will write four essay-style answers. The first answer in worth 40 marks and three answers are worth 20 marks each.

The total examination time is **2 hours and 30 minutes.**

This examination paper is worth 35% of your overall A Level grade.

Exam 1: Component 1: Varieties of film and filmmaking

This examination paper is structured as follows:

Section A: Hollywood film, 1930–1990 (comparative study)

- You will choose one **40-mark** essay question from a choice of two.
- You are expected to **compare the two Hollywood 1930–1990 films** you have studied.
- We recommend you spend **50 minutes** on this section.

Section B: American independent film since 2005 (two-film study)

- You will choose one **40-mark** essay question from a choice of two.
- You will select the **two American films** you have studied for this section. You DO NOT need to compare these films.
- We recommend you spend **50 minutes** on this section.

Section C: British film since 1995 (two-film study)

- You will choose one **40-mark** essay question from a choice of two.
- You will select the **two British films** you have studied for this section. You DO NOT need to compare these films.
- We recommend you spend **50 minutes** on this section.

A Level, Component 2: Global filmmaking perspectives

Section A: Global film (two-film study)

- You will choose one **40-mark** question from a choice of two.
- You will select the **one European film** AND the **one film from outside Europe** you have studied.
- You DO NOT need to compare the two films.
- We recommend you spend **60 minutes** on this section.

Section B: Documentary film

- You will choose one **20-mark** question from a choice of two.
- You will select the **one documentary film** you have studied.
- We recommend you spend **30 minutes** on this section.

Section C: Silent cinema

- You choose one **20-mark** question from a choice of two.
- You will select the **silent film or films** you have studied.
- We recommend you spend **30 minutes** on this section.

Section D: Experimental film

- You will choose one **20-mark** question from a choice of two.
- You will select the **experimental film or films** you have studied.
- We recommend you spend **30 minutes** on this section.

A LEVEL FILM STUDIES Sample Assessment Materials 22

Answer one question from each of Sections A, B, C and D.

You are advised to spend approximately **60 minutes** on your chosen question in Section A and approximately **30 minutes** on your chosen question in each of Sections B, C and D.

Section A: Global film (two-film study)

Answer on one film from group 1 and one film from group 2.

Group 1: European film
- Life is Beautiful (Benigni, Italy, 1997)
- Pan's Labyrinth (Del Toro, Spain, 2006)
- The Diving Bell and the Butterfly (Schnabel France, 2007)
- Ida (Pawlikowski, Poland, 2013)
- Mustang (Ergüven, France/Turkey, 2015)
- Victoria (Schipper, Germany, 2015)

Group 2: Outside Europe
- Dil Se (Ratnam, India, 1998)
- City of God (Mereilles, Brazil, 2002)
- House of Flying Daggers (Zhang, China, 2004)
- Timbuktu (Sissako, Mauritania, 2014)
- Wild Tales (Szifrón, Argentina, 2014)
- Taxi Tehran (Panahi, Iran, 2015).

Either,

1.   (a)   With close reference to the **two** films you have studied, explore how either performance or mise-en-scène create meaning. [40]

Or,

     (b)   With close reference to the **two** films you have studied, explore how either editing or sound create meaning. [40]

Section B: Documentary film

Answer on one of the following documentary films.
- Sisters in Law (Ayisi/Longinotto, Cameroon/UK, 2005)
- The Arbor (Barnard, UK, 2010)
- Stories We Tell (Polley, Canada, 2012)
- 20,000 Days on Earth (Forsyth / Pollard, UK, 2014)
- Amy (Kapadia, UK, 2015)

Either,

2.   (a)   Apply one filmmaker's theory of documentary film you have studied to your chosen documentary. How far does this increase your understanding of the film? [20]

Or,

     (b)   'Portable, digital cameras, digital sound recording equipment and non-linear digital editing have had a very significant impact on documentary film.' How far has digital technology had an impact on your chosen documentary film? [20]

© WJEC CBAC Ltd.

A LEVEL FILM STUDIES Sample Assessment Materials 23

Section C: Film movements - Silent cinema

Answer on one of the following film options.
- Keaton shorts - One Week (1920), The Scarecrow (1920), The 'High Sign' (1921) and Cops (1922)
- Man With a Movie Camera (Vertov, USSR, 1929) and A Propos de Nice (Vigo, 1930)
- Strike (Eisenstein, USSR, 1924)
- Sunrise (Murnau, US, 1927)
- Spies (Lang, Germany, 1928).

Either,

3.   (a)   Discuss how far your chosen film or films reflect aesthetic qualities associated with a particular film movement. [20]

Or,

     (b)   Discuss how far your chosen film or films reflect cultural contexts associated with a particular film movement. [20]

Section D: Film movements - Experimental film (1960-2000)

Answer on one of the following film options.
- Vivre sa vie (Godard, France, 1962)
- Daisies (Chytilova, Czechoslovakia, 1965) and Saute ma ville (Akerman, Belgium, 1968)
- Pulp Fiction (Tarantino, US, 1994)
- Fallen Angels (Wong, Hong Kong, 1995)
- Timecode (Figgis, US, 2000).

Either,

4.   (a)   Explore how far your chosen film or films are experimental in challenging conventional approaches to narrative. [20]

Or,

     (b)   Explore how far cinematography contributes to the 'experimental' identity of your chosen film or films. [20]

WJEC Eduqas Specimen Assessment Materials

AS Level – At a glance: exam paper overview

In the **Component 1** examination, you will write four answers. Section A is worth 60 marks in total and Section B is worth 30 marks in total. The examination is 1 hour and 30 minutes.

In the **Component 2** examination, you will write four answers. Section A is worth 60 marks in total and section B is worth 30 marks in total.

The examination is 2 hours and 30 minutes.

Component 1: American film

This examination paper is structured as follows:

Section A: Hollywood film, 1930–1990 (comparative study)

- You will answer one **20-mark** essay question, then one **40-mark** essay question from a choice of two.
- You are expected to **compare the two Hollywood 1930–1990 films** you have studied in both answers.
- We recommend you spend **60 minutes** on this section.

Section B: American independent film

- You will answer one **10-mark** question, then one **20-mark** essay question from a choice of two.
- You will select the **American independent film** you have studied for this section.
- We recommend you spend **30 minutes** on this section.

Component 2: European film

This examination paper is structured as follows:

Section A: British film since 1995 (two-film study)

- You will answer one **20-mark** essay question, then choose one **40-mark** essay question from a choice of two.
- You will select the **two British films** you have studied for this section. You DO NOT need to compare these films.
- We recommend you spend **60 minutes** on these questions.

Section B: Non-English language European film

- You will answer one **10-mark** exam question, then choose one **20-mark** essay question from a choice of two.
- You will select the **European film** you have studied for this section.
- We recommend you spend **30 minutes** on this section.

Tips: Answering the exam questions

You may be wondering, what you are expected to write in the answer? Don't worry, examiners don't expect all students to answer a question in exactly the same way. You may approach a question in a different way from another student or use different key sequences – that's fine as long as you have answered the question and hit the assessment objectives! It would be very boring if all exam answers were exactly the same.

However, there are some dos and don'ts we suggest you follow when answering a question in the examination.

Do:

- Mention the name of film or films you have studied in the first couple of sentences so that the examiner knows exactly which films you have studied.
- Address the question directly. Leave out any information that does not help you answer the question. You are not expected to write down absolutely everything you have learned about a film. Part of the examination process is your skill to select what is appropriate for a question.
- Use correct film terminology when analysing a key sequence – this helps you be precise and detailed.
- Refer to key sequences. Select key sequences that best help you answer the question.
- Give a brief introduction and conclusion if you have time. These should address the question directly.

Don't:

- Describe the plot of the film in detail. Always assume the examiner is familiar with the film (which they are). Focus on your analysis and answering the question.
- Generalise. It is very easy to talk around the film. Get into the detail of the film through key sequences or key moments.
- Describe theories or feel you have to 'name-drop' theorists. The only area where theory is assessed is in Documentary film through the specialist area of Filmmakers' theories.
- Use the exam to vent your personal thoughts on the film (especially if they are negative). It is not a review of the film. Stay focused on the question.

Practical examination tips

- Use black ink and ensure your writing is readable.
- Write in continuous prose. Only use bullet points if you are running out of time and you need to make a point very quickly before the examination ends.
- Keep an eye on the clock. Follow the recommendations for timings on the 'instructions for candidates' on page 1 and the suggestions on pages 6–7 of the exam paper.
- Double-check you have the correct question number written down at the start of your answer.

Grade booster

Think about what the question is asking you to do. A 'How far'? question will require your judgement based on the evidence you provide. For instance, the question 'How far do the films you have studied reflect their production contexts?' may elicit a range of responses. One student may argue successfully that their chosen films do not reflect their production contexts, while another student may also argue successfully that they do. Always give examples from the films you have studied as evidence for your argument.

How you are assessed: Assessment Objectives 1 and 2

Revision activity

You can write your own mark scheme for any of the practice exam questions in this guide by adapting the marking criteria provided on this page.

Just change the wording so that it is specific to the question you are answering.

Half of the total marks for each question are awarded for **Assessment Objective 1** (AO1). This rewards your ability to **demonstrate** your **knowledge** and **understanding** of the elements of film. Put simply, this Assessment Objective tests what you have learned in class and through your own research.

The other half of the total marks for each question are awarded for **Assessment Objective 2** (AO2). This rewards your ability to critically **apply** your **knowledge** and **understanding** of the relevant elements of film through analysis. Here you should demonstrate how and why films are constructed in particular ways and the meanings and responses they generate.

Knowledge and understanding

It is useful to know the difference between knowledge and understanding in film study.

Knowledge: Key facts you have learned and your knowledge of key sequences.

Understanding: Your ability to explain elements of film and concepts relating to specialist areas. You should be able to provide a detailed analysis of the films to demonstrate you understand key concepts or elements of film.

Marking criteria for a sample question

Let's look at the marking criteria from the Sample Assessment Materials for Component 1: Section B; Question 2b: American film since 2005 (two-film study).

The key terms in the table below are highlighted in bold. Examiners use this when marking your examination response. They need to give three comments directly from the assessment objectives to justify the mark awarded.

How far do your chosen films demonstrate the importance of visual and soundtrack cues in influencing spectator response? Refer in detail to at least one sequence from each film.

Band	AO1 (20 marks) Demonstrate knowledge and understanding of elements of film	AO2 (20 marks) Apply knowledge and understanding of elements of film to analyse films
5	17–20 marks **Excellent demonstration of knowledge and understanding** of the importance of visual and soundtrack cues in influencing spectator response in relation to the chosen films.	17–20 marks **Excellent application of knowledge and understanding** of the importance of visual and soundtrack cues in influencing spectator response to analyse the chosen films. Uses **excellent** points to develop a **sophisticated** exploration of how far spectator responses are influenced by visual and soundtrack cues.

4	13–16 marks	13–16 marks
	Good demonstration of knowledge and understanding of the importance of visual and soundtrack cues in influencing spectator response in relation to the chosen films.	**Good application of knowledge and understanding** of the importance of visual and soundtrack cues in influencing spectator response to analyse the chosen films.
		Uses good points to develop a **detailed** exploration of how far spectator responses are influenced by visual and soundtrack cues.
3	9–12 marks	9–12 marks
	Satisfactory demonstration of knowledge and understanding of the importance of visual and soundtrack cues in influencing spectator response in relation to the chosen films.	**Satisfactory application of knowledge and understanding** of the importance of visual and soundtrack cues in influencing spectator response to analyse the chosen films.
		Uses satisfactory points to develop a reasonably coherent exploration of how far spectator responses are influenced by visual and soundtrack cues.
2	5–8 marks	5–8 marks
	Basic demonstration of knowledge and understanding of the importance of visual and soundtrack cues in influencing spectator response in relation to the chosen films.	**Basic application of knowledge and understanding** of the importance of visual and soundtrack cues in influencing spectator response to consider the chosen films.
		Uses basic points to develop a **partial consideration** of how far spectator responses are influenced by visual and soundtrack cues with little comment on 'how far'.
1	1–4 marks	1–4 marks
	Limited demonstration of knowledge and understanding of the importance of visual and soundtrack cues in influencing spectator response in relation to the chosen films.	**Limited application of knowledge and understanding** of the importance of visual and soundtrack cues in influencing spectator response to consider the chosen films.
		Uses limited points in an attempt to develop a consideration of how spectator responses are influenced by visual and soundtrack cues, with limited/no reference to 'how far'.
	0 marks – **No response attempted** or **no response worthy of credit**.	

Tip: Aim to hit the marking criteria for both assessment objectives. It is possible to gain different marks for each Assessment Objective – e.g. an answer may demonstrate an excellent knowledge of the film (AO1) but a satisfactory ability to apply that knowledge through detailed analysis (AO2).

Revising the core areas: film form

Knowledge booster

The key elements of film form are defined with examples in the textbook on pages 6–47. You can use these pages to help you complete the activities in this section of the revision guide and boost your knowledge of film terminology.

Grade booster

You do not have to define the key elements of film form in your exam answers, e.g. there is no need to state 'mise-en-scène means everything in the scene'. Focus on discussing how particular elements of film form are used in your chosen sequences.

Revision activity

Re-watch the opening sequence from any of the films you have studied. Write a 400-word response to the following question:

How do elements of film form establish the themes, aesthetic and messages in the opening sequence of the film you have studied?

The core areas of film form are:

- **Cinematography, including lighting**
- **Mise-en-scène**
- **Editing**
- **Sound**
- **Performance (A Level only)**.

You should consider the following when revising the core elements of film form:

The core elements: What are the key filmic devices?

The creative use of each element: How do filmmakers use core elements in creative ways to generate meanings and interpretations?

How the core elements convey messages and values: How does the creative use of core elements convey ideologies? How can core elements be interpreted in different ways?

How do core elements work together to create a film's overall aesthetic?

In the examination, you could be asked about how elements of film form relate to other core areas, such as aesthetics, **representations** and **contexts**.

Here are three examples of **practice essay questions** that link film form to other core areas. You can apply these to any of the films you have studied:

- Discuss how two elements of film form contribute to the overall aesthetic of the film you have studied.
- How do mise-en-scène and performance help construct gender representations in the film you have studied?
- How do editing and sound create meaning in the film you have studied?

Activity
Analysing still images from a film

Look at these two shots from the opening sequence of *Bladerunner* (Scott, 1982) and answer the following questions:

- What **shot types** and **camera angles** are used and to what effect?
- How does the **mise-en-scène** establish the genre of the film?
- What type of **lighting** is used and to what effect?
- How would you describe the **aesthetic** of the film based on these two images?

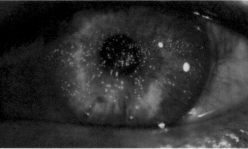

Revising cinematography

When revising cinematography, you should consider:

- Shot types
- Camera angles
- Camera movements
- Lighting
- Composition.

Revision activity

There are some excellent video essays on YouTube which explain aspects of cinematography. We recommend 'Cinematography 101' by Rocketjump Film School as a good introduction to aspects of cinematography. Watch this video and make notes on key terms which aid your knowledge and understanding of cinematography.

Activity
Shot types

Look at the following images from case study films.
Name the shot type and state the common function of this shot type in film:

Shot type:

Function:

Shot type:

Function:

Shot type:

Function:

Activity
Camera angles

State the purpose of each camera angle and give an example from any of the films you have studied. The first example is done for you.

Key camera angle	Purpose	Example
Aerial shot	Bird's eye view. May establish a scene or location.	Apocalypse Now (Coppola, 1979). Aerial shots show the advancement of the helicopters towards the village.
Eye-level shot		
Over-the-shoulder shot		
High-angle shot		
Low-angle shot		

Camera movement

Describe each type of camera movement, state its purpose and give an example from any of the films you have studied. The first example is done for you.

Camera movement	Purpose	Example
Pan Camera is on a fixed axis. Can be moved from left to right or right to left.	Can be used to follow a character or pan across one side of the frame to another.	End of Inception (Nolan, 2010). Camera slowly pans across the room to the spinning top, creating an enigma.
Dolly		
Tracking		
Zoom		
Handheld		
Steadicam		

Direction of lighting

Look at the following images from case study films and answer the following question:

- Where is the direction of lighting in each shot?

You can check the answers on page 17 of the textbook

Composition

Look at this image from *Winter's Bone* (Granik, 2010) and answer the following question:

- How is this image composed? Consider **balance** and **symmetry**, use of the **rule of thirds** and **positioning** of people and objects.

Revising mise-en-scène

When analysing mise-en-scène you should consider:

- Use of colour
- Setting and props
- Costume, make-up and hair
- Staging and movement.

Avoid simply describing what you see in a sequence. Focus instead on how meaning and response are generated by elements of the mise-en-scène.

Think about how mise-en-scène can be used to create **realism** or be used in more symbolic and expressive ways to convey themes and / or the psychology of a character.

Example

In this image from *Secrets & Lies* (Leigh, 1996), mise-en-scène is used to create realism and convey **binary oppositions** as each character's dress codes reflect their differing social class. The character on the left, Hortense, is dressed in professional attire, while the character on the right, Cynthia, is in casual attire.

Revision activity

Look at three still images from a key sequence in one of the films you have studied.

Write bullet points commenting on:

- The use of camera angles and lighting.
- The placement of people and objects within the setting.

Revision activity

Choose one of the films you have studied that was shot in **colour**. Answer the following questions:

1. What are the main colours used to create the overall colour palette?

2. What meanings are generated by the colour palette?

3. How does the colour palette help create the overall aesthetic of the film?

Knowledge booster

Off-screen space

This refers to the areas outside of the frame that the audience imagines. This space is still part of the diegetic world. For example, if a character walks out of the frame to the left, the audience can imagine the character continuing to walk off-screen.

Digital editing

Editing film

Anaylse the use of mise-en-scène in a key sequence from one film you have studied. Answer the following questions:

- How is colour used in the sequence? (E.g. to add to a mood, to signal genre or encourage a psychological response in the spectator.)
- How are setting and props used to help develop narrative and characterisation?
- How are costume and make-up used to develop a character and set the film within a specific time period?
- Where are characters positioned in relation to each other? What does this tell us about their relationship?

Revising editing

When revising editing you should consider:

- The use of **continuity** or invisible editing
- **Experimental** editing, e.g. **montage** editing and continuous takes
- **Shot transitions** – the move from one shot to the next
- The **speed** of editing – the length of each shot.

Answer the following questions (the answers are on pages 30 and 36–37 of the textbook):

1. What is the purpose of continuity editing in mainstream, narrative films?
2. What is the 180-degree rule and why is it used?
3. What is cross-cutting?
4. How does montage editing differ from continuity, invisible editing?
5. What is the Kuleshov effect?
6. How has digital filmmaking aided the use of the continuous take?

Give a definition for each shot transition and state its purpose. The first is done for you (the answers are on page 31 of the textbook).

Transition	Definition and purpose
Cut	*The most common transition. It may not be noticeable. A straight cut from one image to another. Creates a seamless series of shots.*
Fade	
Dissolve	
Wipe	
Match-cut	
Match-dissolve	

Jump-cut	
Freeze-frame	

Activity
Speed of editing

The speed of editing contributes to the pace of a sequence.

- Choose a two-minute key sequence from one of the films you have studied and count the number of shots in the sequence.
- Then count the number of seconds each shot lasts.
- Where do the shots speed up or slow down and to what effect?

Revising sound

When revising the sound, you should consider how the three layers of sound: **dialogue**, **sound effects** and **background** or incidental music, are used to elicit emotion, add realism and draw our attention to specific details.

Activity
Sound – the key terms

Provide a definition for each key term. The first example is done for you:

Key term	Definition
Diegetic	*The sound in the fictional world / the sound characters can hear. Includes vocal and ambient sound.*
Non-diegetic	
Background	
Parallel	
Contrapuntal	
Synchronous	
Asynchronous	

Revising performance

You should consider how different types of performance are used to generate meaning and response. The key elements of performance are:

- **Verbal** and **non-verbal** communication
- Performance **styles**: realist, classical, formalist
- **Acting styles**: improvisation and method acting.

Activity:
Revising sound

Choose a key sequence from one of the films you have studied where there is a lot of sound, including background music. Watch the sequence with the sound turned off. Now watch it again with the sound turned on. Then answer the following question:

How important is sound in generating meaning and response in the film you have studied?

Knowledge booster quiz

Search for the answers online or on page 38 of the textbook.

1. What is a Foley artist?
2. What is the difference between on-screen and off-screen sound?
3. What is ADR?

Knowledge booster

Performance in *Inception* (Nolan, 2010)

Compare the short scene towards the end of the film where Cobb finds an aged Saito in Limbo with the extract from the screenplay for this scene below.

Answer the following question:

- What does Leonardo DiCaprio add to this scene that is not in the screenplay? Think about speech, expression, pose and body codes.

Revision tip

You can do this exercise for all the films you have studied where the screenplay is available online. Try searching the Internet Movie Screenplay Database (imsdb.com) and Simply Scripts (simplyscripts.com).

```
The waves TOSS a BEARDED MAN onto wet sand.

As the Japanese Security Guard turns him onto his back, we
realize that this is Cobb- OLDER. WEARY. TRAVELLED...

INT. DINING ROOM, CASTLE - DAY

Cobb WOLFS his food. The Elderly Japanese Man (Saito, 90
years old) watches him.
                    SAITO
              So... have you come to kill me?

Cobb does not look up.
                    SAITO
              I've been waiting for someone to
              come for me...
                    COBB
              Someone from your half-remembered
              dream...?
Saito peers at Cobb.
                    SAITO
              Cobb? Not possible-he and I were
              young men together. And I am an old
              man...
                    COBB
              Filled with regret?
Saito REMEMBERS, nods...
                    SAITO
              Waiting to die alone, yes.
Cobb is STARING at something on the table.
                    COBB
              I came back for you...I came to
              remind you of what you once knew...
Cobb gestures at the table. Saito follows his gaze down to
the polished surface of the table...
                    COBB
              That this world is not real.


The top IS STILL SPINNING PERFECTLY, AS IF IT WILL NEVER
TOPPLE. Saito looks at the top. Then back to Cobb.
                    SAITO
              You came to convince me to honor
              our arrangement?
                    COBB
              Yes. And to take a leap of faith.
As Saito-san listens to Cobb, he looks at the GUN on the
table between them...
                    COBB
              Come back and we'll be young men
              together again.
The elderly Saito looks at Cobb. Nods. And we-
                                        CUT TO:
```

Knowledge booster

Performance styles

Provide a definition for each performance style and give examples (where relevant) of these styles used in the films you have studied.

Performance style	Definition	Example
Realist		
Classical		
Formalist		

Revising the core areas: representations and aesthetics

Revising representations

You should revise how the following areas are represented in the films you have studied:

- Gender
- Ethnicity
- Age.

Revision tips

- Link your analysis of representations with the films' contexts. For instance, representations of gender are often linked to the social, political and historical contexts in which the film is made. Think about what the film suggests about attitudes to gender and ethnicity at the time it was made.
- Consider what is left out of a film, e.g. a film with an absence of ethnic minority characters may promote whiteness as the 'norm'.
- When discussing representations of ethnicity, don't always assume this only applies to characters from ethnic minorities. Consider whiteness as an ethnicity. How are white characters constructed and represented in the films you have studied?
- Consider how the film's messages are reinforced by the representations.
- When revising key sequences, consider how the representations are constructed through elements of film form, e.g. how a film may light and frame a female character as an object of the male gaze.
- Think about how representations in your films intersect, e.g. how representations of gender may be bound up with other aspects of identity, such as class, ethnicity, sexuality and age.

Sample essay questions on representations

Here are some examples of practice essay questions on representations. You can apply these to any of the films you have studied. Refer to key sequences.

- How is ethnicity represented in the films you have studied?
- How are representations of gender constructed through mise-en-scène and cinematography in the films you have studied?
- How are particular age groups represented in the films you have studied?
- To what extent are the characters stereotyped in the films you have studied?

> **Activity**

Choose one of the above essay questions for any of the films you have studied. Make a five-point plan for how you would approach this essay. Give examples from the film for each point.

> **Activity**

Representations

Some films you have studied may focus on particular issues linking to representations. For instance, *Do the Right Thing* (Lee, 1989) foregrounds racial issues and ethnic minority representations, *Boyhood* (Linklater, 2014) foregrounds representations of age.

Choose five of the films you have studied and state which representations are foregrounded (it may be one, two or all three) and which key sequences you might use in an exam response on representations.

Revision activity

The Bechdel test

To pass the Bechdel test a film has to feature two named female characters who talk to each other about something other than a man. Apply this test to the films you have studied. Give an example of where each film passes the test. You can then cite this in an exam question on gender representations.

Knowledge booster quiz

Go to the website womenandhollywood.com

Look at the statistics for women and Hollywood, then answer the following questions:

1. How many of the top 100 grossing films released last year were directed by women?

2. What percentage of women are moviegoers?

3. What percentage of female characters were white in the top 100 grossing films of last year?

4. Do any of the statistics on this webpage surprise you? What do they tell us about diversity and representation in Hollywood today?

Here is an example of how to complete this activity using *Fish Tank*:

Film	Gender / age / ethnicity	Key sequence
Fish Tank (Arnold, 2009) For British film (two-film study)	**Foregrounds gender and age:** Strong white, working-class teenage girl. More complex representations of teenagers – a rounded character.	**Mia dances with Tyler and Joanne** Mia trying to connect with her mother – a more nuanced portrayal of teen girls. Social realist style with natural lighting and handheld camera gives a more realistic representation.

Film	Gender / age / ethnicity	Key sequence

Knowledge booster

In *Nobody's Girl Friday: The Women Who Ran Hollywood* (2018), historian J. E Smyth challenges our view that years ago there were few jobs for women: 'Between 1930 and 1950, over 40% of film industry employees were women, 25% of all screenwriters were female, one woman ran MGM behind the scenes, over a dozen women worked as producers, a woman headed the Screen Writers Guild three times.'

Task

Research the talent who worked for the studio on your Hollywood studio film. Were there any women producers, scriptwriters and editors who worked on the film or for the studio?

Revising aesthetics

- Consider how all elements of film form work together to create a film's overall aesthetic.
- Link the film's aesthetic to its social and cultural contexts. Consider how the film's aesthetic is indicative of a particular film movement or style.
- Link the film's aesthetic to messages and **ideology**, e.g. *Pan's Labyrinth* (del Toro, 2006) uses the aesthetics of fascism in a twisted, fairy-tale manner to critique this ideology.

- Consider how a film's aesthetic may also be indicative of an auteur signature, e.g. the aesthetic of a psychological, technicolour noir in *Vertigo* is reminiscent of Hitchcock's auteur signature.

Sample essay questions on aesthetics

Here are some sample practice questions on aesthetics. You can apply these to any of the films you have studied. Refer to key sequences in your response.

- How far does the overall aesthetic of the film you have studied reflect the film's cultural and political contexts?
- How do mise-en-scène and sound contribute to the film's overall aesthetic?
- How does the aesthetic of the film you have studied convey themes?

Activity
Aesthetics

Choose one film from the films you have studied and answer the following questions:

- How would you describe the overall aesthetic of the film? Think of at least four adjectives and give examples from the film.
- Choose one frame from a key sequence that is memorable and cinematic. How do the elements of film form work together to construct this striking moment of cinema?
- In what ways does the aesthetic help convey the film's messages and values?

Case study 1: Representations and aesthetics of *This is England* (Meadows, 2006)

This is England critiques post-industrial decline in Britain, demonstrating how far-right groups operate and recruit disaffected young white men – issues which are extremely prescient today. David Buckingham argues that *This is England* '*offers a rich, multi-dimensional narrative of growing up in Thatcher's Britain that takes us beyond the reassurance both of sentimentality and of political oversimplification*' (page 16).

Revision activity

Search online for David Buckingham's essay '*This is England*: Growing Up in Thatcher's Britain'. He describes the film as having 'powerful and distinctive aesthetic style'. Read the essay and make notes on any new insights you gain into the film's representations and aesthetics.

Activity

Representations of gender, age and ethnicity

Answer the following questions on representations in *This is England*.

Give examples from the film to illustrate your points:

- How is the youth subculture of skinheads represented? How does Meadows depict this culture as contradictory and complex?
- How is Shaun represented at the start of the film? How does Meadows use film language to show him as isolated from his peers?
- How is Shaun's mother (Cynthia) represented?
- Even though most of the main characters are white, how does Meadows show that Britain in the 1980s is multicultural?
- How are representations of members of the far-right white nationalist group (e.g. Combo) constructed? How are we meant to feel about them?
- Who or what do you think Meadows blames for the rise of violent far-right groups in England during the 1980s?

Activity

Comparison of father figures

Knowledge booster quiz

Watch the opening 10 minutes of Don Lett's documentary *Skinhead* (available online).

Answer the following questions:

1. When did skinhead culture emerge and what was it a reaction to?

2. What was the relationship between ethnicity and skinhead culture?

3. Describe the visual look of skinheads.

4. Compare images of actual skinheads with representations in *This is England*. Do you think the film offers a realistic visual representation of skinheads?

Compare Shaun's two very different father figures, Woody and Combo. Provide a description of each character and consider how they are represented as binary oppositions. Re-watch the sequences where we see each character in their bedrooms to help you answer the question.

Woody

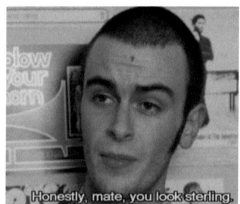

Honestly, mate, you look sterling.

Combo

Activity

Key sequence analysis: The final sequence

Key questions	Analysis
Representations of age	
How does the soundtrack (Clayhill's cover of The Smiths song, 'Please, Please, Please, Let Me Get What I Want') relate to Shaun's journey throughout the film?	

How is Shaun's rejection of nationalistic ideologies reflected in his actions and performance?

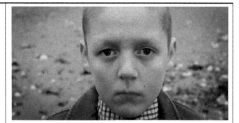

To what extent does the end of the film signal a 'coming of age'? Think about how Shaun is making his own decisions.

Aesthetics

How does Meadows use poetic devices to create an emotional impact?

Watch the final sequence of *The 400 Blows* (Truffaut, 1959). Compare the two sequences. In what ways does Meadows appear to be influenced by this **French New Wave** film about boyhood?

Revision activity

In his chapter summary for 'Twenty-first century social realism', David Forrest argues that 'Contemporary British realism is characterised by a focus on young, marginalised protagonists searching for meaning in poetically charged urban and suburban environments. As such, the representation of landscape, space and place is a persistent source of interest' (online). Write a short 300-word essay answering the following questions:

1. How is location represented in *This is England*?

2. How does this contribute to the film's overall aesthetic?

Aesthetics

In the table below, the first column describes the overall aesthetics of *This is England*. Complete the second and third columns with examples of how the film's aesthetics are constructed and how they are linked to the film's context. Some examples in the second and third columns are given for you.

Aesthetic	How the aesthetics are constructed through elements of film form	How the aesthetics link to contexts and artistic influences
1980s working-class England Poetic realism Social realism Post-industrial decline Skinhead culture Poverty	*Use of soundtrack to evoke the 1980s. Extended montage sequences* *Use of natural lighting* *Real locations*	*Combines elements of art cinema with the social realist films of Ken Loach and Mike Leigh* *Post-war closing of manufacturing industry created high unemployment*

Revising the core areas: the social, cultural, political and institutional contexts of film

The specification says:

Films .... can be understood in more depth by placing them within two important contextual frames. The first involves considering the broader contexts of a film at the time when it was produced – its social, cultural and political contexts, either current or historical. The second involves a consideration of a film's institutional context, including the important contextual factors affecting production such as finance and available technology.

When revising contexts, you should focus on when the film was **made** rather than when it was set.

Contextual areas may overlap and inform each other. The political situation in a society may have an impact on the dominant attitudes and values of a society at the time the film was made. The technological and institutional contexts may be linked, as the filmmakers of a lower budget indie film may respond to technological constraints in creative ways.

Practice essay questions for each contextual area

Below are sample essay questions for each contextual area, with tips on how to approach the essay and each contextual area. You can apply these essay questions to any of the films you have studied. We recommend that you spend 30 minutes answering each essay question.

You can read an example of a practice answer focusing on contexts on pages 38–40 of this revision guide.

Practice essay question: Social contexts

How far does the film you have studied reflect the dominant attitudes and beliefs of the society in which it was made?

Tips

- Consider what was happening in society at the time the film was made. What were the dominant attitudes and beliefs? The films you have studied may uphold dominant beliefs or question them.
- Link social contexts to representations of gender and ethnicity. How a film represents gender and ethnicity may reflect or question a society's dominant values. Think about how a film is a product of the society and culture in which it was made.

Practice essay question: Cultural contexts

How far do popular cultural movements in film and art influence the overall aesthetic of the film you have studied?

Tips

- Culture refers to the way of life, art (e.g. music, art, theatre, literature) and popular art (e.g. film, television, comics, videogames) of a particular society.
- Consider how the films you have studied belong to a particular artistic movement or popular, mainstream style. You might also think about how fashions and customs are reflected in and influence the films you have studied.

Practice essay question: Political contexts

To what extent does the film you have studied engage with the politics of the place and time it was made?

Tips

- Consider the political movements, events and issues taking place at the time the film was made. A filmmaker may seek to comment directly on a political situation to enact a societal change and raise awareness (e.g. Spike Lee's criticism of Mayor Koch in *Do the Right Thing*).
- Some films may have more covert political references, perhaps upholding the dominant ideology and politics of a particular time and place without drawing attention to them.
- Some films may be restricted by the regulation and censorship codes in place at the time they were made.

Practice essay question: Institutional contexts, including production

How far does the film you have studied reflect its production contexts?

Tips

- Consider the institutional frameworks in which filmmakers work. Was the film produced for a major studio or was it an independent production?
- Consider how much freedom filmmakers are given within the institutional frameworks in which they operate.
- What were the unique conditions of production in which the film was made? How do these reflect in the overall look of the film?
- Consider how filmmakers use the technology available to them in creative ways.

We will apply contexts to three case study films from the specification which all feature young women navigating urban city life; *Frances Ha*, *Victoria* and *Vivre sa vie*.

Case study 2: Revising the contexts of *Frances Ha* (Baumbach, 2012)

Knowledge booster quiz

Choose one of the films you have studied. Answer the following questions on the film's **institutional contexts**:

1. How was the film funded?
2. Does the funding impact on how it was made (e.g. budgets, studio-style, etc.)?
3. What was the film's budget?
4. How is the film's budget reflected in its overall style and aesthetic?

Answer the following questions and complete the activities to help you revise the contexts of *Frances Ha*. Use bullet points to note down key points and give examples from the film to illustrate your points.

Social contexts

Key questions

- Define millennials. How are millenials represented in *Frances Ha* through the character of Frances?

- *Guardian* journalist Steve Rose (We've gone through a lot of trauma': why millennial stories are saving Hollywood', *Guardian*, Online, 20 July 2019) discusses some of the issues facing millennials: *'On paper they are the most educated, diverse and materially privileged generation in history but, in the western world at least, millennials are also the first to face dimmer prospects than their elders. Some of them became pop stars and tech entrepreneurs; many more are paying off student debts in dead-end jobs that didn't require a college degree anyway. What's more, they have been guinea pigs in a digital revolution that has transformed civilisation in ways we are still barely getting to grips with.'*
- How are these issues represented in *Frances Ha*?
- How is contemporary New York City represented in *Frances Ha*? What comment does the film make on the experiences of young people living in New York City?

Political contexts

Key questions

- European critics read *Frances Ha* as a comment on class. How can the film be read as a comment on social class? Think about Frances' financial situation, her goals and aspirations.
- Do you think the film celebrates or critiques consumerism and capitalism? Give reasons for your answer.

Cultural contexts

Create a poster which shows how cultural influences impact on the overall style and aesthetic of *Frances Ha*. Use annotated stills from key influences and stills from *Frances Ha* as a visual comparison. Some key influences you can include are:

- French New Wave films, including: *The 400 Blows* (Truffaut, 1959); *Jules and Jim* (Truffaut, 1962); *Breathless* (Godard, 1960); *Vivre sa vie* (Godard, 1962)
- *Manhattan* (Allen, 1979).
- The HBO television series *Girls* (2012–2017).

Institutional contexts

Key questions

- Gerwig argues that *Frances Ha* was 'too risky' for some of the major 'indie' companies such as Fox Searchlight and Sony Pictures Classics. Why do you think the film was deemed 'risky'?
- The film was premiered at film festivals then picked up by IFC films for distribution. Research IFC films. Who are they and why would they choose to distribute *Frances Ha*?
- Research the films of Noah Baumbach and Greta Gerwig. How does *Frances Ha* reflect their auteur signatures as 'indie' writers and directors?
- *Frances Ha* was shot digitally in colour and then transferred to black and white. Baumbach said it was easier and more cost effective to shoot digitally rather than on film. He said transferring it to black and white can 'evoke film but look like something new'. What does the use of black and white add to the film's aesthetic?

- Baumbach and Gerwig noted how they were limited by the cameras they used, as they were not handheld cameras. What does the static camera and smooth shots, rather than handheld, add to the film's aesthetic?

Applying contexts to the opening sequence of *Frances Ha*

Write a 500-word essay on how the opening sequences reflect the film's cultural, social and institutional contexts.

Comment on:

- Cultural influences: French New Wave and *Manhattan.*
- Representations of social groups: young, white, millennial women.
- The 'indie' aesthetic.

Revision activity

The cultural and social contexts of *Frances Ha*

Some audience members have stated online that they found the character of Frances to be unlikeable and frustrating to watch.

1. Give three examples from the film where you feel distanced from Frances.

2. For each example, state how elements of film form are used to create a distancing effect.

3. Give reasons why Baumbach and Gerwig might want us to feel distanced from Frances. Do you think the film suggests that Frances is the cause of her own problems or does the film suggest that wider social and political issues are the problem?

Case study 3: Revising the contexts of *Victoria*
(Schipper, 2015)

Revision activity

Victoria

Watch a scene from *Victoria* without English subtitles. How does this enable you to align yourself more fully with Victoria? What key information does she not hear? Is it easier to understand why Victoria was willing to go along with the heist when you see and hear things from her perspective?

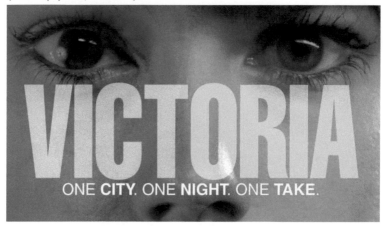

Social, political and historical contexts

Read this extract from an interview with director Sebastian Schipper:

'I wanted this European aspect. I wanted this aspect of Berlin, being a little refuge for people of Europe. The solidarity amongst young people is very touching, they stand for each other, they help each other, and of course, it's no coincidence that she [Victoria] comes from Spain. I didn't want her to come from Greece, because that would make it super political, but obviously she is coming from a place that is not doing so good, and she is coming to a country Germany, and we are doing really, really good.'

Activity

Research the following questions online and write bullet-point answers for each question:

- What happened during the 2008 economic crash?
- What was the impact of the 2008 economic crash on youth employment?
- What is the European Union?

Activity

Use your answers and the extract from the interview with Schipper (above) to complete the following activity:

Re-watch the two short sequences from *Victoria* , described in the table below, where the social and political issues of employment and EU migration are explored. Complete the following table:

Sequence	Examples of how the sequence explores social and political issues
The opening sequence where Victoria talks to the bartender	
The cafe sequence where Victoria talks to Sonne about her financial situation	

Victoria was filmed across 22 locations in the Kreuzberg and Mitte areas of Berlin. Create a poster exploring how Berlin is represented in *Victoria*. Use annotated stills from the film and images of Berlin.

Ensure your poster includes:

- Berlin as the home of European Techno music and 'all-night' clubs
- Berlin as a vibrant, multicultural city
- The social and cultural identity of the Kreuzberg and Mitte areas of Berlin.

Cultural contexts

Key questions

- Consider *Victoria* as a **European art-house** film. Give three examples of how *Victoria* differs from a mainstream film. Think about the style, themes and messages of the film.
- What is **cinéma vérité** and how has this mode of documentary filmmaking influenced *Victoria*?
- Think about the film's **genre**. How does *Victoria* use and subvert the conventions of the **heist movie**?
- How does the aesthetic of *Victoria* reflect the age of the smartphone and social media, where live events can be streamed unedited online?

Institutional contexts

Victoria was shot in one continuous 138-minute take. The film was shot three times and the third take was used. It was filmed at 4am to reduce the chance of people walking into the shot.

Critics made comparisons to other 'one shot' films, *Rope* (Hitchcock, 1948), *Birdman* (Iñárritu, 2014), *Timecode* (Figgis, 2000) and *Russian Ark* (Sokurov, 2002). However, director Sebastian Schipper stated that:

> 'Those films were no reference to us. We were out on the street: our approach was to film the action in the manner of a war photographer. It's not about setting up immaculate framing. You follow an event that is snowballing, and you can't quite believe what's going on, what's going to happen next? You just want to get closer to the action.'

Use the information above and look online for interviews with Schipper and reviews of the film (search online for the *Guardian* and *Sight and Sound* reviews). Answer the following questions:

- To what extent is *Victoria*'s production context a key selling point for the film?
- How does your knowledge of the film's production enhance your appreciation of the film?
- Critic Stephen Holden of the *New York Times* argued that *Victoria* is a 'sensational cinematic stunt'. Give one argument for and one argument against this view that the film is simply a 'stunt'.

Knowledge booster quiz

In 1969, Argentinian filmmakers Solanas and Getino proposed that cinema be broken down into three categories: first, second and third cinema.

Research these categories online and answer the following questions:

1. What are the differences between first, second and third cinema?

2. Do you agree that *Victoria* is an example of second cinema? Give reasons for your answer.

Applying contexts to the opening sequence of *Victoria*

Write or record a commentary on how the **social**, **cultural** and **technological** contexts are reflected in the opening sequences of *Victoria*.

Comment on:

- Berlin's cultural and social identity
- The loneliness for new EU migrants moving to Germany who don't speak German and use English as a common language
- The European Art House and cinéma vérité style.

Case study 4: Revising the contexts of *Vivre sa vie* (Godard, 1962)

Revision activity

Research **Jean-Luc Godard** as a filmmaker and watch clips from some of his most influential films, including *Breathless* (1960) and *Une femme est une femme* (1961).

Answer the following questions:

1. How would you define Godard's auteur signature style?

2. What was Godard's relationship to Anna Karina and how is this relevant for understanding the production contexts of *Vivre sa vie?*

Social and political contexts

Key questions

- How does *Vivre sa vie* represent Paris during the early 1960s? Think about the places Nana frequents.
- Consider Godard as a left-wing filmmaker. What political comment does he make about the treatment of women and sex workers in Paris?

Cultural and institutional contexts

Create a poster which shows the key cultural influences on the overall style and aesthetic of *Vivre sa vie*. Use annotated stills from key influences and stills from *Vivre sa vie* as a visual comparison. Some key influences you can include are:

- *The Passion of Joan of Arc* (Dreyer, 1928)
- The aesthetics of director Robert Bresson's films, including *Diary of a Country Priest* (1951) and *A Man Escaped* (1956)
- Playwright and director Bertolt Brecht
- Hollywood genre cinema of the 1940s and 1950s, e.g. film noir.

Note down examples of where we see these influences in *Vivre sa vie*.

Activity

Film movements: French New Wave

Create a **knowledge organiser** on French New Wave cinema. Look for examples of knowledge organisers online to help you structure your own.

Your knowledge organiser should be two sides of A4. Include the following information:

- The defining characteristics of French New Wave films
- A timeline of key French New Wave films
- Images from key films and filmmakers
- A list of reasons why French New Wave filmmakers were motivated to make unconventional films.

Activity

Vivre sa vie as an art film

We can consider *Vivre sa vie* as an example of art cinema. Film historian David Bordwell's essay 'Art Cinema as a Mode of Practice' identifies the key characteristics of art cinema.

Look at this list and identify which characteristics apply to *Vivre sa vie*. Give examples from the film for each characteristic. The first example is completed for you.

Key characteristics of art cinema	Examples from *Vivre sa vie*
A realistic cinema with use of real locations	*Shot on location in Paris. Use of cafes, bars and streets in central Paris*
Narratives are explicitly against the classical narrative mode. Looser narratives and looser sense of cause and effect. Narratives have a drifting, episodic quality	
Psychologically complex characters dealing with real problems	
Characters may lack defined desires and goals	
A cinema of reaction rather than action – focus on psychological effects and their causes	
May have a documentary factuality and/or an intense psychological subjectivity	

Revision activity

Search online for the 'WJEC Eduqas *Vivre sa vie* Student resource'. Complete the activities in this resource. You can then search for 'WJEC Eduqas *Vivre sa vie* Teacher Resource'. This provides possible answers for the activities in the student guide. You can use this to help revise other key sequences in the film and the contextual areas.

Violations of classical film time and space – e.g. jump-cuts, plot manipulations of story order	
Stylistic devices such as the long take, the moving camera and deep focus may be employed	
Foregrounding of the film's author/auteur – the director has creative freedom	
The viewer expects stylistic signatures rather than order in the narrative	
Viewers encounter the film and auteur through film festivals, essays, reviews, film education	
Auteur signatures manifest through violations of classical cinema	
An ambiguous cinema, reflecting character ambiguity, the author's signature and 'life's untidiness'	

Activity

Applying social, cultural, political and institutional contexts to Tableau 8 of *Vivre sa vie*

This is the most sociological scene in the whole film. The montage and voice-over give us a glimpse into the realities of life and work for Parisian sex workers. Raoul's dialogue is based on a 1959 sociological account of prostitution in Paris.

Watch the sequence, then answer the following questions using bullet points:

- How does Godard use montage and documentary techniques and to what effect?
- What do we learn about sex work in Paris? How does Godard represent the treatment of sex workers in Paris?
- What does Raoul's **narration** reveal about how women are treated and how their beauty can be used for profit? What do you learn about changes in the law and requirements for medical checks?
- How is sex work as a clinical, business encounter reflected in the use of editing, cinematography, mise-en-scène and sound?

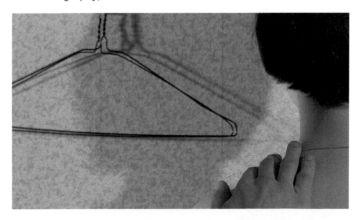

Hollywood 1930–1990, comparative study

What to revise

The core areas:

- **Film form**: cinematography, mise-en-scène, sound, editing and performance
- **Representations** and **aesthetics**
- Comparison of the films' social, cultural, historical and institutional (including production) **contexts.**

The specialist area:

- **Auteur**

This is the section of the examination where you are assessed on your **comparison** of the two Hollywood films you have studied. Your comparison should focus on the films' **contexts**. Consider how Hollywood during the **studio system** (1930–1960) was different from Hollywood after the studio system (1960–1990) in terms of production, technology, political, cultural, social and historical factors.

Apply your knowledge of the films' contexts to key sequences.

In the examination you will be given a choice of two questions worth 40 marks each. Answer one of the two questions. We recommend that you spend 50 minutes on this question, including planning time.

> **AS Level:** The specialist area of auteur is not assessed in the AS exam.
>
> You will answer two questions, applying the **core areas only** to your two chosen films. Question 1.a. is worth 20 marks. You will then be given a choice of two 40-mark questions (questions 1.b or 1.c). You are expected to compare the films you have studied.

Key questions

The Hollywood studio system

1. What was the **1948 Paramount Decree** and what impact did it have on the major Hollywood studios?
2. What is **vertical integration**?
3. Who were **the Big Five** and **the Little Three** studios?
4. What was a **movie mogul**?

Grade booster

Ensure you explicitly compare both films in your examination response. You can use key terms such as 'Both (insert film titles)' and 'In comparison'.

Revising the contexts of Hollywood, 1930–1990

Activity

Complete the following table to help you revise and compare the different contexts of Hollywood during the studio era and the period of **New Hollywood** after the studio era. The first two examples are completed for you.

Focus	Studio system	After the studio system
Audiences	Large, mass audiences. Audiences reach a peak in 1946 with 80 million American citizens attending the cinema.	Fragmentation. More targeting of specific demographics – e.g. young people in the late 1960s. Audiences decline due to changing leisure pursuits – e.g. TV, move to the suburbs, car ownership.
Structure	Vertical integration. The Big Five and the Little Three. Studios have a house style. Key personnel on contract. Factory line methods of production. Studio moguls in charge of the studios.	Break-up of the major studios in the 1950s after the 1948 Paramount Decree. 1980s – Blockbuster era and return to industry control of a small number of global conglomerates. Talent signs contract for one film or franchise.

Stars		
Auteurs		
Technology		
Censorship		

Key questions

Studio house style

For your chosen film from the studio era, research and answer the following questions:

1. Which studio produced the film?

2. Did the studio have a 'house style' at the time of your chosen film's production? Was it famous for certain genres and stars?

3. Who was the studio head/mogul at the time of production? Who was the film's producer? Do they contribute to the overall style of your studio film?

Revising auteur

Auteur is the French word for author. This is from the idea that for a film to be viewed as a work of art, it must therefore be assigned an artist or creator.

Your chosen films may have an auteur director with a distinctive style. We must consider, however, that film is also a collaborative effort. Other key personnel such as the editor, composer and cinematographer may also contribute to the overall aesthetic, themes and messages of your chosen films. Today, the term auteur is used loosely to describe filmmakers who have a signature style.

Tip: While you do not have to 'name-drop' auteur theorists to gain marks in the exam, it is worth understanding how the auteur theory developed, from *Cahiers du Cinéma* critics of the 1950s who elevated certain Hollywood directors during the studio era, to Andrew Sarris' essay 'Notes on the Auteur Theory' (1962).

Revising auteur as a critical approach

Tip: You should evaluate the usefulness of auteur as an approach. Think about how an auteur approach has increased your understanding of Classical Hollywood and New Hollywood and the insights you have gained from comparing the auteurs of the two films you have studied. You should also consider the limitations of auteur as an approach. Think about how other approaches (e.g. a contextual approach) offer different insights and understandings of the two films you have studied. The following activity will help you evaluate an auteur approach.

Activity

Evaluating an auteur critical approach

Search online for critic Pauline Kael's essay 'Circles and Squares' (1963). This essay is a famous critique of Andrew Sarris' 'Notes on the Auteur'. Read the essay and make notes on her critique of the auteur theory. You can use these arguments to help critically evaluate the auteur theory.

Then write bullet points listing the usefulness and limitations of the auteur approach to films. Try to find at least three points for each. Give examples from the films you have studied to illustrate your points.

Auteur during the Hollywood studio system, 1930–1960

The studio era problematises the notion that the director is a film's sole author. Often the studio head or 'mogul' and the producers were the most powerful people who oversaw production and hired key talent, such as directors, editors and cinematographers. However, for the *Cahiers du Cinéma* critics, there were some powerful directors working within a studio system with a clear authorial trademark across their body of films. These auteur directors included Alfred Hitchcock, Orson Welles and John Ford.

Alfred Hitchcock

A Level practice question

'The overall style of a film is determined by the director.' Compare how far is this true for the films you have studied.

Answer this question using the two Hollywood 1960–1990 films you have studied.

- Set a timer for 50 minutes to practise exam timings.
- Refer to key sequences.
- Look at the mark scheme in the WJEC Eduqas Specimen Assessment Materials (online) and assess your own work.
- Consider swapping essays with a fellow student and marking each other's response.

Case study 1

Casablanca (Curtiz, 1942) and *Bonnie and Clyde* (Penn, 1967)

Comparing the contexts of *Casablanca* and *Bonnie and Clyde*

Complete the table to compare the contexts in which the two films were produced and released. The first example is completed for you.

Context	*Casablanca*	*Bonnie and Clyde*
Social, political and historical	*World War II. America is at first reluctant to enter into the war – isolationist. They enter after the surprise Japanese attack on Pearl Harbor on 7 Dec. 1941.*	*Vietnam War (1955–1975). Countercultural movement which opposes war – mainly younger people. People seeing graphic, violent images of war on television and in newspapers.*
Financial		

Knowledge booster

List the key conventions of the classical Hollywood style. Now give examples from the New Hollywood film you have studied where these conventions are broken. State the purpose and effect of breaking these conventions.

Key questions

1. Define the 180-degree rule and explain its purpose.
2. What is **continuity editing** and why is it commonly used in classical Hollywood films?

Consider the key talent on each film who, working together, contributed to the overall look of them.

For each key talent, write a sentence describing their auteur trademark.

Casablanca:

Executive producer Jack Warner

Producer Hal B. Wallis

Director Michael Curtiz

Cinematographer Arthur Edeson

Composer Max Steiner

Institutional		
Production		
Cultural		
Technological		

Comparison of key scenes 1: introduction of the main characters

The best way to compare your films is through a close analysis of key sequences. This will ensure you stay focused on the film and link the contexts and specialist area of auteur to the core areas.

Do not simply describe what you see in a sequence, e.g. this is a close-up shot. You should also discuss the meaning of the cinematic devices used, e.g. 'The use of the extreme close-up on Bonnie's lips in the opening sequence of *Bonnie and Clyde* reflects the French New Wave style in New Hollywood films of the late 1960s, which broke away from the classical Hollywood style.'

We will first compare the opening sequence of *Bonnie and Clyde* with the sequence in *Casablanca* where we first meet Rick in Rick's Café Americain. Then we will compare the final sequences of both films.

You can apply the comparisons of these two sequences to any sequences from the films.

Core areas

Film form

Classical Hollywood style: Give examples where *Bonnie and Clyde* is influenced by French New Wave, defying the classical Hollywood. Contrast these with examples of how *Casablanca* follows conventions.

Give examples where *Bonnie and Clyde* uses a conventional classical Hollywood style of editing.

Are there examples of the following in both sequences?

- The 180-degree rule
- Shot/reverse shot for conversations
- Establishing shots
- Invisible editing.

Compare the **lighting** – e.g. low key vs high key. What is the impact of the different lighting styles in both films?

Performance: Consider examples of how Bogart performs the character of Rick as a world-weary, isolated character in this sequence. How do Rick (Bogart) and Clyde (Beatty) offer different types of masculinity? How does this reflect social and historical changes at the time the films were made?

Representations

How does the opening of *Bonnie and Clyde* establish Bonnie as a woman who does not want to be domesticated in a traditional role?

How is **ethnicity** represented? Consider Rick's bar as a refuge for different ethnic groups escaping Nazi persecution.

How is **age** represented? Consider Rick as an older more cynical character in comparison to the younger characters or Bonnie and Clyde?

Contexts

How are the typical styles and influences of the **historical periods** when the films were made reflected in these sequences?

In *Casablanca*, look at the exact date where Rick signs the cheque. Why is this date significant?

In *Bonnie and Clyde*, how is Bonnie introduced as a woman who is rebellious and seeks excitement? How and why would this appeal to younger audiences in 1967?

How does *Bonnie and Clyde* reflect a more liberal attitude to on-screen nudity in this opening sequence?

Specialist area of auteur

How does this sequence in *Casablanca* exemplify the studio house style of Warner Brothers in its use of stars (Bogart), cinematography (Arthur Edeson) and use of music?

Now compare this to *Bonnie and Clyde*. How does the sequence reflect Dede Allen's editing style and director Arthur Penn's preference for location shooting?

Revision activity (cont'd)

Bonnie and Clyde:

Director Arthur Penn

Screenwriters David Newman and Robert Benton

Editor Dede Allen

Producer Warren Beatty

Choose two of your own comparable sequences from each film. You might want to choose a climatic or emotional moment from each film.

Apply the core areas and specialist area of auteur. Write a 200-word analysis comparing the two sequences.

Knowledge booster quiz

Contexts

Casablanca

1. Why does Renault throw the bottle of Vichy water in the bin?

2. What was the resistance and which character embodies the resistance movement?

Bonnie and Clyde

1. What was the counterculture?

2. When was President John F. Kennedy assassinated and how is this referenced in the film?

Comparison of key sequences 2: final sequences

Re-watch the final sequences of both *Bonnie and Clyde* and *Casablanca*.

Film form

Compare the **editing** styles of both sequences. How do the rapid, fast cuts in *Bonnie and Clyde* contrast with the more invisible, conventional editing style in *Casablanca*? What is the impact of these two editing styles on the spectator?

Mise-en-scène: Location – consider how this sequence in *Casablanca* was shot on a studio lot, with the use of fog to disguise the set, whereas this final sequence in *Bonnie and Clyde* was shot on location outdoors in Texas. Do you think on-location shooting makes *Bonnie and Clyde* more realistic?

Sound: How is sound and music (or lack of) used in these sequences?

Compare the final moments of both films. How do both films give a sense of closure in different ways?

Contexts

Arthur Penn has said that he was able to show more extreme violence as people were desensitised to violence after watching footage of the Vietnam War on their TV screens. How is this reflected in the depiction of violence in the final sequence of *Bonnie and Clyde*?

These final sequences in *Casablanca* are full of messages to the American audience that they should be involved in the war effort. Give examples of dialogue and imagery which demonstrate the need for self-sacrifice and loss and different countries allying together.

Sample essay comparing the production of *Bonnie and Clyde* and *Casablanca*

A short but relevant introduction with clear comparison and demonstration of knowledge (AO1)

Direct comparison of use of settings, linking to production contexts of studio filmmaking vs location filmmaking

While both *Casablanca* and *Bonnie and Clyde* were produced for the major Hollywood studio Warner Brothers, *Casablanca* was produced at the height of the studio era, whereas *Bonnie and Clyde* was produced in the period of 'New Hollywood' (1967–1974), when the major studios were no longer vertically integrated.

Casablanca reflects the studio-bound production of the studio era, where films were produced in-house on studio lots. Even though the film is set in Casablanca, Morocco, only realistic stock footage of location is used in the opening sequences, whereas the location is recreated on the Warner Brothers' studio lot to enable more control of the production and to allow producer Hal B. Wallis and executive producer Jack Warner to oversee production. The final sequences exemplify the expertise and style of Warner Brothers and the collaborative nature of studio filmmaking. The use of fog disguises the studio set. Depth and perspective are provided by using a miniature plane which, in the long- and mid-shots where Rick and Isla say goodbye, looks like it is in the distance, while Rick and Isla are in the foreground of the shot. Even the final line of dialogue, 'this is the beginning of a beautiful friendship', reflects the collaborative nature of studio production of the 1940s, as it was written by producer Hal B. Wallis.

In contrast, director Arthur Penn chose to shoot *Bonnie and Clyde* on location in Texas not only to add a realism to the film, reflected in the dusty landscapes and colour scheme of browns and yellows, in keeping with the influence of French New Wave films, which made use of locations, but also for Penn to keep away executive producer Jack Warner so that he could make the film he wanted without too much studio interference.

Detailed analysis comparing two key sequences

Stylistically, *Casablanca* exemplifies the norms of classical filmmaking of the 1940s, typical of the ways in which such films were produced. The sequence where we first meet Rick is typical of the classical Hollywood style. The scene begins with a long establishing shot depicting the exterior of Rick's Café American, shot on the studio lot, to establish location. The interior shots first establish space though tracking shots, then cut into medium close-ups of characters of different ethnicities in the bar, a typical way to shoot a sequence in the classical period. The cinematography, particularly the use of low-key lighting, is a stylistic device common in films of the 1940s as Warner's embraced a tough, gritty style in line with the popularity of film noir hardboiled detective stories. We see this in the same sequence when we first meet Rick, as he sits alone in a medium close-up with low-key lighting used to help convey his cynicism and isolation.

In contrast, *Bonnie and Clyde* reflects the changes in style in New Hollywood cinema of the late 1960s. The use of an extreme close-up of Bonnie's lips at the start of the scene also reflects the trend in production to defy the norms of classical filmmaking. However, *Bonnie and Clyde* does not totally depart from the Hollywood style. It is, after all, still a Hollywood production. The sequence where Bonnie first sees Clyde from her bedroom window is at times shot in a conventional way, using continuity editing and shot/reverse shot.

Both *Casablanca* and *Bonnie and Clyde* reflect censorship and regulation at the time of production. *Casablanca* was produced at a time when scripts would adhere to the production code, a form of self-censorship where films would have to adhere to a set of rules. Scripts would be sent to the Hays Office (who administered the code) for approval. *Casablanca* adheres to the Hays code as there is no direct reference to sex during scenes of Rick and Isla's romance in Paris. *Bonnie and Clyde* reflects the changes in attitudes of the late 1960s, appealing to a younger audience with a more liberal attitude towards sex and violence on screen.

Comparison of the changes in censorship and regulation

By 1967 the production code was outdated, and Penn made the decision to leave in the scene where Bonnie attempts to perform oral sex on Clyde, even though it violated the code. References imply that Clyde is impotent as he says 'I ain't no loverboy'. The more liberal attitudes towards more explicit violence on screen is best exemplified in the final sequences of *Bonnie and Clyde*, where their deaths are violent and bloody. Penn thought that audiences were now desensitised to violence, as they had watched footage of the Vietnam War nightly on television. The scene and the film end abruptly, as a shot of Bonnie and Clyde's killers is viewed through a car window which has been shot through by a bullet then suddenly cuts to black with no fade or pan out. This reflects the changes in New Hollywood films, which were influenced by European Art House films which would deliberately end more abruptly to produce a sense of shock. This abrupt ending contrasts to the conventional studio ending of *Casablanca* where the orchestral music swells, with a long-shot of Rick and Renault walking into the distance.

Application of knowledge applied to key final moments of the two films

Overall, *Casablanca* and *Bonnie and Clyde* reflect their different production contexts. *Casablanca* is reflective of 1940s studio filmmaking, while the experimentation on *Bonnie and Clyde* helped usher in the period of New Hollywood, which broke away from some of the norms and restrictions of studio filmmaking.

Finish it

Complete the following practice 40-mark question comparing *Casablanca* and *Bonnie and Clyde*. The first short paragraph is written for you. Aim to use two key sequences from each film.

Compare how far your chosen films reflect their auteur signatures

To an extent, *Casablanca* reflects the auteur signature of Warner Brothers as a studio with a 'house style' and the collaborative nature of studio filmmaking, while *Bonnie and Clyde* reflects the signature of director Arthur Penn and also other key talent on the film, such as editor Dede Allen and screenwriters Newman and Benton. This essay will explore how key talent who can be classed as auteurs work collaboratively to create the overall look and messages of the films using two key sequences from each film to demonstrate this.

AS Grade booster

Advice for 20-mark answers:
- Aim to write at least one side of A4.
- Spend between 20 and 25 minutes on your response.
- Refer to a key sequence from each film.
- Keep your introduction short and to the point.
- Ensure you answer the question directly.

A brief introduction introducing and comparing the two films

Detailed focus on a specific sequence

Direct comparison

Focused on a key sequence
Use of relevant film terminology

AS Level: Hollywood 1960–1990, comparative study

AS Level essay comparing sound and editing in *Casablanca* and *Bonnie and Clyde*

In *Casablanca*, sound and editing is in the classical Hollywood style and heightens the sense of romance and nostalgia. However, *Bonnie and Clyde* is more experimental in its use of sound and editing, typical of New Hollywood films of the late 1960s.

The final sequences of *Casablanca* employ continuity, invisible editing and an orchestral, non-diegetic score. The sequence in which Rick and Isla say goodbye cuts from a two-shot of Rick explaining to Isla that she must leave with Laslo to a series of shot/reverse shots to enable the audience to focus in on their responses, this cuts to a tighter close-up of Isla as she realises the sacrifice she must make after Rick utters the film's most famous line 'here's looking at you kid' and enables the audience to empathise with her. The leitmotif of 'As Time Goes By' plays non-diegetically to heighten the sense of nostalgia, romance and now loss. When Isla walks off with Laslo, in a medium long-shot, this orchestral version of 'As Time Goes By' is imbued with a darker tone to reflect the sadness of the situation and heighten the spectator's emotional response to Rick's sacrifice. In contrast, the final sequences of *Bonnie and Clyde* use only heightened diegetic sounds. Rapid jarring cuts between Clyde, Malcolm and Bonnie are used as they hear the diegetic sound of frightened birds flying away. This sound of the birds foreshadows their own sudden deaths in the seconds that follow. The use of silence punctuated with the heightened bird sound, then the rapid sound of gunfire, makes Bonnie and Clydes' deaths seem even more sudden, violent and shocking.

In *Bonnie and Clyde*, editor Dede Allen was influenced by more experimental European films which used jump-cuts and sharp transitions from close-ups or extreme close-ups to a long shot. This is reflected in the death sequence which is composed of around 50 shots which transition between rapid edits. The edits then slow down at the end of the sequence and slow motion is used to give a stylised, impactful portrayal of their deaths as Bonnie and Clydes' bodies are flung about due to the rapid gunfire. The use of silence over the final shot and title card is deliberate to allow their deaths to sink in but to also not encourage us to sympathise with them too much, in contrast with our sympathy towards Isla and Rick, as Bonnie and Clyde are not traditional Hollywood heroes, they were criminals on a killing spree. In contrast, *Casablanca* ends with a typical Hollywood long-shot over the swelling of the orchestral score. This creates closure and also promotes the film's propagandistic message of the need to join forces with the resistance and fight the war. The film's message of the need to sacrifice and make allies is exemplified in the film's final line as Rick says to Renault, 'Louis, I think this is the beginning of a beautiful friendship'.

The use of sound and editing in the of ending in each film differs, reflecting the times in which the films were made, with *Casablanca*'s reflecting studio production while *Bonnie and Clyde* is more experimental in its use of sound and editing, ushering in the new Hollywood style of the late 1960s.

Detailed analysis

Direct comparison

A short conclusion

Finish it

Complete the following practice exam question response using *Casablanca* and *Bonnie and Clyde*. The first paragraph has been written for you. Spend about 20 minutes on your answer. Compare a key sequence from each film.

Points to consider:

- Comparison of Isla and Bonnie
- Consideration of social and cultural contexts
- How representations are constructed through elements of film form.

Compare the representations of gender in the two films you have studied.

Casablanca represents traditional ideals of masculinity through the character of Rick, and Hollywood notions of femininity and beauty through the character of Isla. In comparison, *Bonnie and Clyde* reflects the more sexually liberated era of the late 1960s with the character of Bonnie and, to a certain extent, challenges traditional ideals of masculinity with the character of Clyde.

Vertigo (Hitchcock, 1958) and *Do the Right Thing* (Lee, 1989)

Alfred Hitchcock and Spike Lee as auteurs

Both *Vertigo* and *Do the Right Thing* are personal, complex, 'masterpiece' films by their respective auteur directors. Hitchcock and Lee produced *and* directed their films, maintaining creative control. Hitchcock is an example of an auteur director working within the studio system, while Lee reflects New Black cinema of the late 1980s/early 1990s, when black filmmakers such as Spike Lee and John Singleton responded to racial injustices and inequality from a black perspective. We will consider both Hitchcock's and Lee's auteur trademarks and the collaborative nature of filmmaking by considering the key talents they worked with to help achieve their visions.

> **Activity**
> ### The auteur signatures of Hitchcock and Lee
>
> Compare the auteur signatures of Alfred Hitchcock and Spike Lee. Give examples from *Vertigo* and *Do the Right Thing* to illustrate your points. The first example is started for you.

	Alfred Hitchcock	Spike Lee
Themes and issues	*Freudian psychology* *Blonde women as victims/in peril* *Guilt* *Voyeurism* *Duality*	*Multicultural tensions, often between black and Italian Americans* *Police brutality and white supremacy*
Institutional contexts		
Representations – gender/ethnicity/age		

Revision activity

The production contexts of *Do the Right Thing*

Search online for the hour-long documentary *Making 'Do the Right Thing'* (St. Clair Bourne, 1989). Apply your knowledge and understanding of the film's production to a key moment or sequence.

Do you agree that the film downplayed the drug problems and offered a sanitised version of the real location?

Revision activity

Auteur and *Vertigo*

Hitchcock wanted to create 'pure cinema'. Research what is meant by pure cinema and give examples of this in *Vertigo*.

Visual style		
Genres		

Activity

Key talent on *Vertigo* and *Do the Right Thing*

Vertigo

Vertigo is notable for its soundtrack, iconic title sequence and costume design. Research and make notes on the following talent who contributed to *Vertigo* and examples of where and how their signature style is evident in the film.

Key talent	Signature style	Examples in *Vertigo*
Graphic designer Saul Bass		
Composer Bernard Herrmann		
Costume designer Edith Head		

Do the Right Thing

Spike Lee directed, produced, wrote and starred in *Do the Right Thing*. He also collaborated with accomplished talents to achieve his goal in making a politically charged film. Consider how the film's effective cinematography, editing and soundtrack contribute to the film's overall aesthetic and messages.

Key talent	Signature style	Examples in *Do the Right Thing*
Cinematographer Ernest Dickerson		
Editor Barry Alexander Brown		
Composer Bill Lee (created the jazz score)		
Rap group Public Enemy (title track: 'Fight the Power')		

Knowledge booster

Political contexts of *Do the Right Thing*

Research the following real-life people and incidents:
- Mayor Koch
- The Tawana Brawley case
- The Howard Beach incident.

Where and how are all these incidents referenced in the film?

Knowledge booster

Find out about the backgrounds of Hitchcock and Lee. How do their childhood experiences and early careers inform their filmmaking?

Revision activity

Do the Right Thing ends with quotations from Martin Luther King and Malcolm X. Research the ideologies of these two important figures in the fight for equality.

Why do you think Lee chose to show both their perspectives at the end of the film?

Contextualising *Vertigo* and *Do the Right Thing*

Revision activity

Research how critics responded to *Vertigo* and *Do the Right Thing* when they were first released. Were the films held in such high regard as they are today? Did they cause any controversy upon release?

Revision activity

Read the following statements:

'*Vertigo* is a deeply misogynistic film.'

'*Do the Right Thing* trades on outdated racial stereotypes.'

Write one argument for and one argument against each of these statements. Give examples from the films as evidence for your points.

Activity

Complete the following table comparing the institutional, political, social, cultural and historical contexts of *Vertigo* and *Do the Right Thing*. Give examples from the films to apply your knowledge and understanding to key sequences or moments. Each section is started for you.

Context	*Vertigo*	*Do the Right Thing*
Institutional (including production)	Major stars James Stewart and Kim Novak	No major stars. Low budget
Political and historical	Cold War anxieties	1980s Reaganism Mayor Koch in New York City (NYC)
Social and cultural	Pre-feminist society	Popularity of Rap music

Comparison of key sequences: *Vertigo* and *Do the Right Thing*

Key sequence 1: opening sequences (including title sequences)

Compare the opening sequences of *Vertigo* and *Do the Right Thing* by answering the following questions on core areas and auteur.

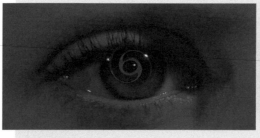

Revision activity

Re-watch the final sequences of *Vertigo* and *Do the Right Thing*. Write a 400-word analysis comparing the use of film form, representations, contexts and auteur trademarks in these two sequences.

Core areas:

Film form

Key question: How do both sequences establish the films' themes and issues?

Aesthetics

How would you describe the overall aesthetics of both films? How is this established in the opening scenes?

Mise-en-scène

How is colour used in an **expressionist** manner in both title sequences?

Which colours do we associate with Midge and Scottie in *Vertigo*?

How does colour reflect the heat and rising tensions in *Do the Right Thing*?

What recurrent motifs are established in both scenes?

How do both scenes establish settings and use of locations?

Cinematography

How do both sequences use camera angles and movement to establish characters, themes and the overall aesthetic?

Sound

Compare the opening soundtracks, Saul Bass's score over the titles and Public Enemy's 'Fight the Power'. How do the soundtracks establish the films' themes?

Do the Right Thing: What is meant by the first line of the film 'Wake up!'?

Representations

Both sequences open with images of a woman. How do they use women to establish themes? Consider how, after the title sequences, both sequences establish male characters as the main characters.

The first female character in *Vertigo* is Midge. How is she represented as a mother figure to Scottie and how does she differ from the character of Judy/Madeline?

How does *Do the Right Thing* establish issues of racial tension and black visibility?

Contexts

How do these opening sequences reflect the style of filmmaking at the time of production?

How is *Do the Right Thing* overtly political in the title sequences and through the introductions to characters DJ Love Daddy, Smiley and Mookie? What do we learn about each character?

Auteur

How do the opening sequences of both films reflect their respective auteur signatures?

Key sequences 2: Judy becomes Madeline and the confrontation at Sal's pizzeria

Compare the sequence in *Vertigo* where Judy becomes Madeline with the sequences in *Do the Right Thing* where Radio Raheem and Buggin' Out confront Sal in the Pizzeria and the killing of Radio Raheem. Answer the following questions.

Revision activity

Read the BFI Classics books on *Vertigo* (author: Charles Barr, 2nd edition, 2012) and *Do the Right Thing* (author: Ed Guerrero, 2001). Highlight or make notes on any section of the books which increases your knowledge and understanding of the following areas:

- Film form
- Representations
- Contexts
- Auteur.

Revision activity

Read pages 51–59 of the textbook. These pages focus on representations in *Vertigo* and *Do the Right Thing*.

Make notes or highlight the key points in this section.

Use these notes and your sequence analysis to answer the following essay question:

Compare the representations of gender and ethnicity in *Vertigo* and *Do the Right Thing*.

Film form

How are power relationships established in both scenes through **cinematography** and **mise-en-scène**?

Vertigo: How does this sequence suggest that Scottie is descending into a fantasy world? How is this sequence an example of pure cinema?

Do the Right Thing: How do the main characters convey the rising tensions through their **performances**?

How are swirling and circular motifs used in this sequence?

How does **editing** create tension in both sequences?

How is **sound** used in both scenes to create intensity and tension within the characters and their relationships?

Representations

Compare the representations of **gender** in these sequences. Consider who has the power and agency in these sequences.

How do representations of gender intersect with **ethnicity** and **age** in *Do the Right Thing*?

Do you think the younger characters' age in *Do the Right Thing* affects their responses to their situation and each other? How do they differ from the older characters?

Contexts

How does *Do the Right Thing* deal with issues of racial tension and police brutality in these sequences?

Consider how Lee shows this from the perspective of young black residents. How does this contrast to how news media would portray such events?

How can this sequence in *Vertigo* be read as men trying to reassert their dominance over women in post-war USA?

Auteur

How do these sequences reflect Hitchcock's and Lee's auteur signatures?

Revision activity

Search online for 'Eduqas A Level Component 1 Hollywood Comparison Study Guide'. Download '*Vertigo* and Auteur study sheet' and '*Vertigo* and Context study sheet'. Complete the activities provided in these documents.

Revision activity

Compare how *Vertigo* and *Do the Right Thing* use long tracking shots, often on location, in different ways. Give examples of where these tracking shots are used.

Sample essay comparing auteur in *Vertigo* and *Do the Right Thing*

Vertigo (Hitchcock) and *Do the Right Thing* (Lee) were directed by auteur director/producers. While Spike Lee had to accept a lower budget for *Do the Right Thing* from Universal than was usual for a Hollywood production, he had final cut approval and agreement on the casting. Hitchcock marketed himself as the main creator of his films, appearing on posters and cameos in each film. *Vertigo* is considered to be his masterpiece, the ultimate example of his trademarks, including an obsession with blonde women, themes of guilt and Freudian psychology and imagery.

Hitchcock learned his craft in silent cinema and developed methods of 'pure cinema' where he could tell a story visually and through the formal grammar of film. In *Vertigo*, there are long stretches of film where Scottie follows Madeleine around with no dialogue. Instead we focus on Scottie's expression and the point of view shots as we witness Madeline as voyeurs ourselves, blurring the lines between subjective and objective camera. One of Hitchcock's trademarks is his use of subjective shots, giving us the point of view of a particular character. This is evident in the opening sequences of *Vertigo* where Scottie clings to a collapsed gutter on the roof. Hitchcock deploys a dolly zoom to convey the sensation of vertigo. The camera moves towards the ground while zooming out, which distorts perspective. This also reflects Hitchcock's trademark of filmic experimentation.

Application of knowledge to a key sequence

This experimental style of filming is also evident in *Do the Right Thing* as the visual style and editing of it is typical of Lee, where he zooms away from one character and cuts to another to give a juxtaposing viewpoint. This is evident in the scene where the characters all break the fourth wall and speak to camera. This montage is used to reflect the racial tensions in the neighbourhood, as the characters use racial slurs. Lee employs Dutch angles throughout and these, combined with close-ups, build up the oppressive heat which is symbolic of the tensions building to the climactic riot.

Comparison of the two auteur signatures with examples from a key scene

Spike Lee's politics, highlighting racial injustices and inequality, are at the forefront of *Do the Right Thing*. Racially charged incidents in NYC affected the messages of the film, as Lee hoped the film would convince black voters in NYC to vote out the Mayor, Ed Koch. In one scene in the film, graffiti can be seen on the wall which reads 'Dump Koch'. Spike Lee therefore challenged the white hegemony of Hollywood production by making challenging films about the black experience using black actors and crew. One key scene is where Mookie complains about the lack of black people in Sal's 'wall of fame' at the pizzeria, which is a comment on the lack of black representation in the media at that time.

Auteur signatures linked to political contexts

For Hitchcock, it was his fascination with Freudian psychology that came to the fore in *Vertigo* through the theme of voyeurism, dream imagery, a fascination with death (the death wish) and obsession. Hitchcock exploited the voyeuristic nature of cinema and would often put the spectator in the position of voyeur. In *Vertigo*, when Scottie first sees Madeleine at Ernie's restaurant, the camera moves away from Scottie and slowly towards Madeline. We now become the voyeurs. When we cut back to Scottie's point of view, as he gazes at Madeline from a distance, she is framed within frames, a recurrent motif typical of Hitchcock's films, where characters are contained within mirrors and frames. This links to another of Hitchcock's auteur signatures, the use of doubling or doppelgangers. This is used here as Scottie tries to recreate Judy as Madeleine. He sees her in silhouette cast against the green, ghostly light outside. Here Judy resembles Madeleine and Scottie can project his obsession with Madeleine onto Judy. Scottie's obsession with Madeleine and insistence on making up Judy as Madeleine also reflects Hitchcock's own control and obsession with his blonde female stars.

Detailed analysis of a key sequence with use of relevant film terminology

As film is a collaborative medium, it is not only the director who contributes to the overall aesthetic of a film. Spike Lee worked closely with the composer, his father Bill Lee, whose nostalgic and melodramatic jazz score links the film to deeper black American culture and musical roots.

Composer Bernard Herrmann worked with Hitchcock for 11 years, scoring his most famous films such as *Psycho* and *Vertigo*. *Vertigo*'s score is swirling and romantic, yet haunting, reflecting love yet also the sensation of falling. Herrmann's score in *Vertigo* enhances the subjectivity. When Scottie sees Madeleine for the first time at Ernie's restaurant, we hear the romantic and lyrical Madeleine motif as the camera moves closer to her, reflective of Scottie's instant love for her. The musical motif is used again when he refashions Judy as Madeleine. Judy/Madeleine appears as a ghostly image. The score is cyclical and repetitive, reflecting the circular imagery of the film such as downward spirals and the eye and Scottie's own despair and spiral into mental illness.

Awareness of the collaborative nature of filmmaking

This sequence also exemplifies Hitchcock's trait of taking us into the mind of the character through a subjective camera, giving us the perspective of a psychologically scarred character.

A short conclusion

Vertigo and *Do the Right Thing* reflect directors who had a great deal of agency on their films and therefore the films' style and themes reflect their auteur signatures.

Finish it

Complete the following practice 40-mark exam question response using *Do the Right Thing* and *Vertigo*. The first short paragraph is written for you. Aim to use two key sequences from each film.

> **How far do the two films you have studied reflect their political and social contexts?**

Do the Right Thing explicitly reflects its production context, as Spike Lee intended the film to be overtly political. As a classical Hollywood film, *Vertigo* does not have overt political messages. It instead reflects the cultural and social fascination with Freudian psychology and implicitly upholds dominant ideals through its all-white cast and lead male protagonist. It reflects some social male anxieties in post-war USA.

Revision activity

Create your own 20-mark questions for the comparative study by replacing 'sound and mise-en-scène' with two other aspects of film form – e.g. 'Compare the use of **performance** and **editing** in the two films you have studied.'

AS Level

AS Level: Hollywood 1960–1990, comparative study

AS Level essay comparing sound and mise-en-scene in *Vertigo* and *Do the Right Thing*

Both *Vertigo* (Hitchcock, 1958) and *Do the Right Thing* (Lee, 1989) use sound and mise-en-scène in highly expressive and symbolic ways. In *Vertigo* there are moments of 'pure cinema' where narrative is told purely through visual imagery and the non-diegetic score to explore complex themes of obsession and voyeurism. In *Do the Right Thing*, sound and mise-en-scène exemplify issues of racial injustice and rising tensions in the multicultural neighbourhood of Bed-Sty, Brooklyn.

Lee uses Public Enemy's 'Fight the Power' throughout *Do the Right Thing* as a musical motif. The politically charged lyrics, which challenge white hegemony, resonate with Lee's anti-authoritarian stance. The track is first used non-diegetically over the title credits as Rosie Perez dances defiantly in a highly stylised Brooklyn street bathed in reds and oranges, a reference to Lee's love of stylised musical films. The track is then used diegetically through the character of Radio Raheem who plays it on his boombox, as his music is often his 'voice'. The lyrics 'Elvis was a hero to most but he never meant shit to me', which deals with the lack of black representations and elevating of white artists, links to the mise-en-scène in Sal's Pizzeria with Sal's 'wall of fame', which feature no black heroes. The character of Buggin Out complains that there are no 'brothers on the wall' as a montage of images in Sal's wall of fame show mainly Italian Americans such as Al Pacino and Robert De Niro. Buggin Out reminds Sal that it is mainly black Americans spending money at the pizzeria, reflecting the lack of black representation in film and media at the time of the film's production, as black consumers are not represented, yet pay money into the system. Later, when Raheem and Buggin Out return to Sal's, 'Fight the Power' is used as a political act to demonstrate them attempting to assert their identity and culture in the pizzeria. Sal's destruction of Radio Raheem's boombox and the subsequent moments of silence as the characters are stunned by Sal's outburst leads to the subsequent destruction of Sal's Pizzeria.

The introduction immediately introduces and compares the two films

Knowledge of how music is used to convey issues

Detailed sequence analysis

Music is also used symbolically in *Vertigo*, mainly through Bernard Herrmann's non-diegetic score, which reflects Scottie's growing obsession and twisted love for 'Madeleine'. This non-diegetic score is heightened in the scene where Judy 'becomes' Madeleine. She enters the door bathed in a ghostly green light, a symbolic colour used throughout the film to represent Scottie's obsession with what he thinks is a ghost and also Judy's envy of Scottie's twisted love of Madeleine. The music swells, becoming more intense and manic, matching the swirling camera as Scottie is momentarily lost in his ghostly illusion. Musical notes ascend and descend like a carousel, continuing the circular, swirling motifs.

Costume and location are important elements of the mise-en-scène in *Vertigo* and *Do the Right Thing*. In *Do the Right Thing*, costume conveys the characters' identities. For instance, Mookie wears a Jackie Robinson Brooklyn Dodgers baseball shirt. This is significant as Jackie Robinson was the first black player to play Major League Baseball, another nod to black heroes not represented in Sal's wall of fame. In *Vertigo*, Hitchcock specifically requested that costume designer Edith Head create a grey suit to make it look like Madeleine has just stepped out of the San Francisco fog. Madeleine's grey suit gives her an icy, mysterious and stiff demeanour. This is reflected in Kim Novak's performance, as she appears in the ghostly light looking uncomfortable and rigid in the suit. The use of actual San Francisco landscapes and landmarks, with its twisting streets and hills, reflects the swirling, twisted nature of Scottie. In *Do the Right Thing*, the use of a real street in the location of Bed-Sty, Brooklyn, where all the action is contained, lends the film a realism and contributes to the claustrophobic atmosphere. The painting of the buildings in reds and oranges is used expressively to contribute to the theme of heat and rising tensions in the heatwave.

Overall, sound and mise-en-scène are integral elements in portraying the themes and issues of *Vertigo* and *Do the Right Thing*.

Application of knowledge to a key sequence.

Direct comparisons with detailed examples from both films

A brief conclusion

AS Level

Finish it

Complete the following practice exam question response using *Do the Right Thing* and *Vertigo*. The first introductory paragraph has been written for you. Spend about 20 minutes on your answer.

Compare a key sequence from each film.

Points to consider:

- *Do the Right Thing*: representations of Tina in the opening sequence and the 'ice cube' sequence.
- *Vertigo*: how Madeleine is represented from Scottie's point of view in the sequences where he follows her around the city.

Compare the representations of gender in the two films you have studied.

Both *Vertigo* and *Do the Right Thing* have been criticised for their portrayals of women, subjecting them to a male gaze and only viewing women from the perspective of men. However, there are moments in both films that complicate the notion than women are simply passive objects.

American film since 2005 (two-film study)

Knowledge booster

Ideological critical approach

Refers to how we might analyse a film from a particular critical perspective – e.g. a feminist or political perspective.

What to revise

The core areas:

- **Film form**: cinematography, mise-en-scène, sound, editing and performance
- **Representations** and **aesthetics**
- Social, cultural, political, historical and institutional (including production) **contexts**.

The specialist areas:

- **Spectatorship**
- **Ideology**.

How you will be assessed at A Level

- In the examination, you will choose one question out of a choice of two.
- The question is worth **40 marks**.
- You are assessed on your knowledge and understanding of the two American films you have studied.
- Use the film you have studied from group one and the film you have studied from group two.
- You could be asked a question about the specialist areas of spectatorship and ideology.

How to approach a 40-mark question on American film

- We recommend that you spend 50 minutes maximum answering the question (including planning time).
- You do not need to compare the films.
- Focus on one or two sequences from each film.
- Link the specialist areas of spectatorship and/or ideology to your close analysis of the films.
- You are not expected to know or name-drop theorists' names (if you have been taught them).
- You do not need to describe or explain any theories related to spectatorship and ideology. Focus on applying them to the film.

AS Level

What to revise

The core areas:

- Film form: cinematography, mise-en-scène, sound and editing
- Representations and aesthetics
- Social, cultural, political, historical and institutional (including production) contexts.

The specialist area:

- Spectatorship

In the examination, you will answer one question worth **10 marks**, then choose between two questions worth **20 marks**.

We will firstly revise the specialist areas of spectatorship and ideology with activities you can use with any of the American films you have studied. We will then revise two case studies from Group 1: *La La Land* and *Carol* and two case studies from Group 2: *Beasts of the Southern Wild* and *Captain Fantastic*.

Approaching the specialist areas of spectatorship and ideology

Revising the specialist area of spectatorship

The specification says:

> '*Films are generally constructed to provide the spectator with a particular viewing position, most often aligning the spectator with a specific character or point of view. This in turn raises questions about how 'determined' spectators' responses to a film are and how far spectators can and do resist the position they are given. Learners will thus consider how far spectators are 'passive' or 'active' in their responses to film and how social and cultural factors, as well as the specific viewing conditions in which a film is seen, influence spectators' responses.*'

You should revise the following areas of spectatorship:

- How the spectator interacts with film narrative and elements of film.
- Reasons for the uniformity or diversity of response by different spectators.
- The impact of different viewing conditions on spectator response.
- The analysis of narrative, visual, musical, performance, genre and auteur cues in relation to spectator response.
- The possibility of preferred, negotiated, oppositional and aberrant 'readings' of film.
- Active and passive spectatorship.

Revising the specialist area of ideology

The specification says:

> '*The concept of film as ideological involves exploring what ideologies are conveyed by a film as well as those which inform it which may, for example, reveal that a film reinforces or challenges dominant beliefs and attitudes within a society.*'

You should revise the following areas of ideology:

- The ideological connotations of elements of film form.
- Binary oppositions, the use of formal elements contained both in the narrative and those in films.
- How the spectator is positioned and addressed.
- Ideological perspectives appropriate to the film (such as a feminist or a political perspective).
- An **evaluation of the ideological critical approach** to film.

Tip: We advise you to revise spectatorship and ideology together. Spectatorship and ideology are closely linked, as the ideological lens through which we view a film may determine our response to it. For instance, a film that depicts women as passive objects, when viewed from feminist ideological approach, may encourage a feminist spectator to have an oppositional reading of the film.

Grade booster

In an examination response on **spectatorship and ideology**, stay focused on the film using key sequences. Focus on the film's messages and values and how these are conveyed using the core elements of film form.

Revision activity

Search on the WJEC Eduqas website for 'What is Ideology? Student Guide'. Complete the activities in the guide to help you revise ideology in American film.

Activity

Spectatorship and ideology: key terms and concepts

Provide a definition for the following key terms and concepts relating to spectatorship and ideology:

Key term/concept	Definition
Character **alignment**	
Preferred reading	
Negotiated reading	
Oppositional reading	

Revision activity

Ideology in American film

Often, key messages and values are evident in the final sequences of a film, where characters are rewarded or punished for their actions or learn lessons.

Re-watch the final sequences of the two American films you have studied. Write a 500-word essay analysing how the ending of each film conveys key messages and values through elements of film form.

Activity

Applying spectatorship and ideology to American film

Answer the following questions on spectatorship and ideology using the two American films you have studied. Give specific examples from the films to illustrate your points.

- What are the main messages and values of the films?
- Do the films reinforce, challenge or reject the dominant attitudes of the society within which they were made? Give examples from the films to illustrate your points.
- Which main characters are the audience encouraged to align or identify with and why?

Activity

Spectatorship and ideology in American film: critical responses

Search online for critical responses to the two films you have studied. Find a range of responses, including critics and spectators who are critical of the film. Look at reviews, YouTube videos, podcasts and online articles about the films.

Bullet point your key observations on each film, discussing the differing critical responses to each film. Comment on:

- Was there a range of differing responses or were critics/reviewers mainly unanimous in their responses to the films?
- The reasons why some critics/reviewers may have been critical of aspects of the film.
- The lens through which the critic/reviewer was viewing the film – e.g. a feminist critique.
- How the critical responses you have read and listened to may have challenged or reaffirmed your own views of the film.

Activity

Evaluating ideological critical approaches

Write a 1000-word essay on the following question:

Evaluate how far the ideological critical approaches have been useful in developing your response to the films.

Ensure your response addresses the following:

- Refer to at least one ideological critical approach you applied to each American film you have studied (e.g. a capitalist approach, a feminist approach).
- Address the 'how far' aspect of the question – give your own spectator response. Your response to the film may be enhanced through an ideological critical approach. You could also argue that one approach is more useful to you than another.
- Apply the two ideological critical approaches to relevant key sequences.
- Consider how your spectator response is shaped by the core areas of film form.

La La Land (Chazelle, 2016)

Revising the core areas of film form and aesthetics in *La La Land*

Activity

Key sequence: 'Another Day of Sun'

We will apply the core areas of film form and aesthetics to the opening sequences of *La La Land*. If possible, watch the opening sequences with the subtitles on so that you can read the radio announcements at the start of the film and pay attention to the lyrics of the song 'Another Day of Sun'.

Write or record an audio commentary for the sequence, analysing the core areas and the overall aesthetic of the sequence.

Use the bullet points below to help you structure your commentary.

Cinematography

- Fluid camera movement
- Use of wide shots
- Use of crane shots
- How space is established
- **CinemaScope**.

Mise-en-scène

- Use of costume
- On-location shooting in Los Angeles (LA).

Watch sequences from the video essay *Los Angeles Plays Itself* by Thom Andersen (2003). Then write a 300-word essay with visual images analysing how Los Angeles is represented in *La La Land*. Compare and contrast it to the representation of Los Angeles in other films explored in *Los Angeles Plays Itself*.

Revision activity

La La Land is an example of a Hollywood film about Hollywood film.

Other examples include:

Sunset Boulevard (Wilder, 1950)

The Player (Altman, 1992)

Hail, Caesar! (Coen Brothers, 2016)

Once Upon a Time in Hollywood (Tarantino, 2019).

Create a poster with annotated stills from *La La Land*, illustrating how Hollywood represents itself in the film.

Sound

- How the radio announcements establish time and place
- How the song 'Another Day of Sun' establishes themes and mood.

Editing

- The illusion of a single take
- How the sequence is edited to the beat of the song.

Performance

- The switch between realist performances and musical performances.

Aesthetics

- How the sequence replicates classical musicals
- The use of primary colours – and how the film homages Technicolor films.

Activity

Film form and aesthetics

Compare aspects of film form in the opening sequence of *La La Land* with the sequence shot in a more realist mode where Mia and Seb argue while eating dinner. Note down the contrasts between the opening and the dinner sequence. The first example is completed for you.

Film form	Opening sequence	The dinner sequence
Mise-en-scène	*Bright, primary colours and costumes* *On location – expansive, sunny LA*	*More muted colours* *Studio set indoors* *Claustrophobic atmosphere*
Cinematography		
Sound		
Editing		
Performance		

Revising representations and spectatorship and ideology in *La La Land*

Activity

Representations of ethnicity and the specialist area of ideology

La La Land has been criticised for its under-representation of black and Latino people, therefore not reflecting the ethnic diversity of LA.

Search online for the article 'The Unbearable Whiteness of *La La Land*' by Geoff Nelson in pastemagazine.com.

Read the article then answer the following questions:

- What arguments does Nelson make to critique the lack of ethnic diversity in *La La Land*?
- How does Nelson link the nostalgic elements of the film to current US politics?
- How far does viewing the film through the lens of racial politics change your own response to the film? Do you agree or disagree with Nelson's arguments?
- Do you think that Mia's and Seb's white, middle-class privilege make them less relatable as characters?

Activity

Representations of gender and spectatorship

Read this extract from the WJEC Eduqas factsheet on *La La Land*:

'*Some have criticised the gender politics in the film, accusing it of being a male fantasy about artistic integrity (Seb's struggle with the lure of the commerce) that Mia just facilitates and applauds (there are a lot of scenes of her watching Seb perform, very few of him watching her).*

However, another view is proposed by Anna Leszkiewitz, in a New Statesmen article: that actually the film is shot mostly from Mia's perspective. Initially, Seb seems the 'creative' one – unable to play Christmas carols without drifting into his own virtuoso compositions, whilst Mia recites dumb movie dialogue whilst trying to put her soul into 2-dimensional roles. She seems more audience than creator. Yet that, Leszkiewitz says, is to unfairly dismiss being an audience member as a passive role. La La Land, *she suggests, is a film that celebrates the audience experience: Mia may be a spectator for Seb, but she revels in the experience of consuming art: jazz, cinema, cheesy 80s pop, theatre. Cutaways to her dancing or cheering (even her dance to Seb's 80s cover band) show her joy in being an audience member.*'

Revision activity

Gender in *La La Land*

Answer the following short essay question:

To what extent does Seb conform to traditional ideas of masculinity?

Refer to key moments or sequences from the film to illustrate your points

Revision activity

Performance in *La La Land*

Re-watch the audition sequence ('The Fools who Dream') in *La La Land*.

Write or record a commentary on Emma Stone's performance in this sequence. Include how filmic devices are used to intensify her performance.

- Use these arguments and your own analysis of the film to argue for and against the representation of Mia as a passive female character.
- Give three points or examples for each argument.
- Consider how a feminist reading of the film may change your own response to the film? Do you agree or disagree with criticisms of gender politics in the film?

Activity
Representations of age

Mia and Seb are represented as young adults in their 20s, trying to establish their careers. Indeed, one of the key themes of the film is growing up. Think about how Seb and Mia change throughout the course of the narrative. Write a short 300-word analysis of how age is represented in the film.

Use the bullet points below to help guide your analysis:

- Stereotypical ideas of people in their 20s
- Seb and Mia as characters who experience growth and change
- How the film perpetuates nostalgic ideas of first love
- How the film represents issues facing young adults, e.g., choosing between a career and relationships.

Revising the contexts and specialist areas of *La La Land*

Revision activity

The political contexts of *La La Land*

Research the American Dream as an ideology, then answer the following questions:

1. What is the key belief of the American Dream?

2. Give examples of how *La La Land* promotes the American Dream.

3. Give examples of how *La La Land* critiques the American Dream.

Activity
Cultural contexts

La La Land is full of intertextual references and homages to the musical genre and the classical Hollywood era.

Create a poster with images from *La La Land* and the films it references.

Refer to images from the following films to get you started:

- *Singin' in the Rain* (Donen, 1952)
- *The Umbrellas of Cherbourg* (Demy, 1964)
- *Casablanca* (Curtiz, 1942)
- *Rebel Without a Cause* (Ray, 1955).

Key sequence analysis: final sequences

Write an analysis either in essay form or as bullet points on the final sequences of *La La Land*, applying the core and specialist areas. Use the bullet points and images below to help guide your analysis.

Revision activity

Read the sample response on *La La Land* on page 141 of the textbook. Write an extra paragraph using a different key sequence to the response.

Core areas:

Film form

- How a sense of melancholy and romantic loss is reflected in the mise-en-scène and cinematography
- The use of montage editing during the fantasy sequences
- The use of deliberately stylised and artificial sets to evoke fantasy
- The use of musical motifs – Seb's motif on the piano and the medley of songs heard throughout the film
- The sense of romantic loss expressed in Mia's face during the close-up as she watches Seb on the piano.

Representations

- How the scene represents the characters who have grown up, yet still fantasise about young love.

Contexts

- References to classic musicals during the musical sequence, including *An American in Paris* and *Singin' in the Rain*
- References to the ending of *Casablanca* with the sense of nostalgia for the past and romantic loss.

Specialist areas:

Spectatorship and ideology

- The film's ideological comment on the artifice of Hollywood – how it offers fantasies of happy endings and undercuts the notion of the American Dream
- How the film reinforces dominant ideologies of white, heterosexual romance as the norm
- How our alignment shifts between Mia and Seb and evokes empathy with both characters.

Carol (Haynes, 2015)

The **Vito Russo test** is designed to assess representations of LGBTQ+ characters in films. Research the test online and answer the following questions:

1. What is the Vito Russo test and why was it developed?

2. How can the test help determine how LGBTQ characters are represented?

3. Apply the test to *Carol*. Does the film pass the test?

Revision activity

Find and watch documentaries on the history of LGBTQ cinema, including *Gay Hollywood: The Last Taboo* (2009) and *The Celluloid Closet* (Epstein and Friedman, 1995).

Write a short summary of how Hollywood has traditionally represented or excluded LGBTQ+ characters.

Revising the core areas of *Carol*

> Activity

Film form and representations of gender

Re-watch the short scene where Therese photographs Carol shopping for a Christmas tree. Annotate the following three images from the sequence, applying the core areas.

Use the bullet points to help guide your analysis:

Image	Analysis
	■ The use of obscured screens and reflections
	■ Viewing Carol through Therese's lens ■ Use of shot/reverse shot
	■ How small gestures appear erotic ■ The use of colour – e.g. red ■ How the scene subverts the male gaze

Representations of gender, age and sexuality

Look at this image of women in an American print advert of the 1950s:

Search for other images of women in 1950s print adverts. Use these adverts and your knowledge of *Carol* to answer the following questions:

- How were women represented in American advertising during the 1950s?
- How do the representations of women in *Carol* contrast with these images?
- How does *Carol* represent the 1950s as a time of conformity, where sexuality outside of the heterosexual family unit is not accepted?
- What comments does the film make on how women who transgress heteronormative (the belief that heterosexuality is the norm) society are treated?

Cultural and political contexts

Todd Haynes is a prolific filmmaker in a movement film academics and critics refer to as **New Queer Cinema**. Search 'New Queer Cinema' online for articles, definitions and analysis of this movement. Then answer the following questions:

- What is New Queer Cinema?
- During which era did New Queer Cinema develop and why?
- Who are some of the key filmmakers of the movement?
- What are some of the themes of New Queer Cinema films?
- Why are 'queer' films and themes more prevalent in American independent cinema than in mainstream American cinema?

Todd Haynes

Cultural contexts and aesthetics

Create a poster displaying artistic and filmic influences Todd Haynes used to create the overall aesthetic of *Carol*.

All that Heaven Allows (Sirk, 1955)

Include:

- The films of Douglas Sirk
- New York photographers of the 1950s: Ruth Orkin, Esther Bubley and Saul Leiter
- The paintings of Edward Hopper
- Hollywood female stars of the studio era – Lauren Bacall and Audrey Hepburn.

Revision activity

Search online for the GLAAD Studio Responsibility Index at GLADD.org.

Click on 'Overview of Findings'. Answer the following questions:

1. What do the findings reveal about the representation of LGBTQ characters in major studio releases?

2. Are the numbers of LGBTQ films increasing or decreasing?

3. Which genres and studios are the most inclusive?

Revision activity

Todd Haynes was influenced by the British film *Brief Encounter* (Lean, 1945). Watch the film and note down how the film influenced *Carol*. Refer to the use of filmic devices, performance, story and narrative structure.

Revising the specialist area of spectatorship in *Carol*

Activity
Spectatorship

Answer the following questions on spectatorship in *Carol* using bullet points.

- Which character or characters do you align most with in *Carol*? Explain how particular sequences are constructed to encourage you to align with particular characters.
- Are there any points in the narrative where your alignment shifts from one character to another? Give examples from the film.
- How are you encouraged to feel towards Harge? How is Harge constructed to emphasise the messages of the film? Think about how he represents a conformist American society.

Activity
Evaluating ideological critical approaches

Choose two **ideological critical approaches** you have studied in relation to *Carol*.

Create a PowerPoint presentation which explains, evaluates and applies the ideological critical approach to *Carol*.

Include the following in your slides:

- An explanation and definition of the ideological critical approach you studied (e.g. queer theory, feminist approach).
- Apply each approach to *Carol*. Refer to key sequences and the critical responses to the film which view it through a particular ideological lens.
- Evaluate how useful the approach is for understanding the film.
- Give your opinion on which approach out of the two you found the most useful and why.

Key sequence analysis: Therese and Carol first meet in the department store

Re-watch the sequence where Therese and Carol first meet in the department store. On the NY Times YouTube channel, watch the video 'Anatomy of a Scene: CAROL by Todd Haynes' where he discusses this sequence.

Write or record an audio commentary for the sequence, focusing on the core and specialist areas.

Use the bullet points and the 'Anatomy of a Scene' video to help structure your commentary.

Mise-en-scène

- Use of muted greens and blacks
- The symbolism of the train set
- The importance of costume
- Use of frames around characters
- The narrative and symbolic significance of the gloves.

Cinematography

- Use of static shots
- Use of diagonal tracking shots.

Revision activity

Search on the 'Digging Deeper' YouTube channel for the video essay 'Carol: The love story in a look'. Watch the video and answer the following questions:

1. How is colour used symbolically in *Carol*?

2. What is the symbolic meaning of the toy train? How does this compare to its symbolic meaning in the book *Carol* is based on, *The Price of Salt* (Patricia Highsmith, 1952)?

Sound

- Lack of a non-diegetic score
- Coded dialogue.

Editing

- Use of shot/reverse shot and 180-degree rule
- Cut from slow tracking shot to the close-up of Carol's gloves.

Performance

- Use of subtle glances and gestures.

Contexts and ideology

- Characters 'boxed in' - suggests a repressive society
- Comparisons to Douglas Sirk's melodramas.

Spectatorship

- How we are aligned with Therese.

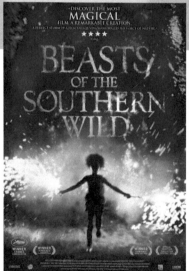

Case study 3

Beasts of the Southern Wild
(Zeitlin, 2012)

Revising the core areas of film form in *Beasts of the Southern Wild*

Key sequence analysis: the opening sequences

Write or record an audio commentary on the use of film form, aesthetics and spectatorship in the opening sequences of *Beasts of the Southern Wild*.

Use the following questions to guide your analysis.

- How are elements of film form used to portray the Bathtub as an isolated place?
- Hushpuppy describes the Bathtub as 'the prettiest place on earth'. How is this depicted through mise-en-scène and cinematography?
- How is the 'dry world' represented?

- What filmic devices are used to align us with Hushpuppy?
- How does Hushpuppy's voice-over establish character and themes?
- How would you describe the overall aesthetic of the film and how is this aesthetic established in the opening sequences?
- The filmmakers wanted to show a place that is different from the rest of America. How is this established in the opening sequences?

Activity

Aesthetics

Beasts of the Southern Wild has been described by critics as combining the following aesthetics:

- Nature documentary
- Social realism
- **Magic realism**
- Poetic realism
- Post-apocalyptic fiction.

Create a PowerPoint presentation analysing the aesthetics of *Beasts of the Southern Wild*. On each slide, provide a definition of each of the above styles/modes of filmmaking.

Give examples of how *Beasts of the Southern Wild* combines and utilises these styles/modes.

Use images from the film in your slides.

Activity

Representations of gender and age

Re-watch the short sequence where Wink encourages Hushpuppy to be tough, asking 'who the man?' and the sequence where Hushpuppy is in the sports arena in a traditionally feminine dress and hairstyle.

Compare the representations of Hushpuppy as a young girl in these two scenes. Discuss how the film aligns us to Hushpuppy as a tough, independent young girl, defying stereotypes. Think about how you respond as a spectator when you see Hushpuppy in the dress.

Sequence: Who the man?	Representations:

Sequence: Hushpuppy in a dress	Representations:

Revision activity

On YouTube, watch the video 'The Cinematography Behind *Beasts of the Southern Wild*', where Director of Photography, Ben Richardson, discusses the film's cinematography.

Answer the following questions:

1. What was Richardson's approach to shooting the film?

2. What were the main inspirations for the look and style of the film?

3. What types of lens did the filmmakers use and why?

4. How did the filmmakers capture Hushpuppy's sense of the world?

Knowledge booster quiz

Answer the following questions about *Beasts of the Southern Wild*'s relationship to the Sundance Film Festival. The answers can be found on pages 145–146 of the textbook:

1. What is the Sundance Film Festival?

2. What is the Sundance Institute Directors Lab Program?

3. Which prize did *Beasts of the Southern Wild* win at the Sundance Film Festival?

Representations of ethnicity

Some critics, including *Time Out* critic Ben Kenigsberg, have argued that the film plays on outdated stereotypes of black Americans: *'the largely black residents are depicted as alcoholics, inattentive parents or fools'*. However, *Guardian* critic Peter Bradshaw argued that in the film *'semi-feral poverty has rendered racial distinctions irrelevant'*.

- Write an argument for and against these statements, using examples from the film. Then state which argument you agree most with and why.

Political contexts, spectatorship and ideology

The magazine *The New Republic* accuses *Beasts of the Southern Wild* of sentimentalising poverty:

> *'Beasts does something more pernicious than simply celebrate poverty. In casting social workers and public health officials who presume to think that a six-year-old girl should be fed, clothed, and looked after by adults as villains, the film tells us that we needn't worry, that the poor just want to be left to fend for themselves. This is the film's ugly operating assumption: if you are already poor (being black doesn't hurt either), you are uniquely suited to thrive in squalor.'*

Use this opinion-piece and your own analysis of the film to answer the following questions:

- How does the film portray poverty? Do you think it sentimentalises poverty and demonises charity workers?
- How do the characters respond to charity efforts? Why are they so reluctant to leave the Bathtub?
- Hushpuppy describes the sports arena as an 'empty fish tank'? How are filmic devices used to portray this sense of a sterile environment and an 'empty fish tank'? How does it compare to the vivid natural life of the Bathtub?
- How far has reading this ideological view of the film influenced your own response to the film? Do you agree with *The New Republic* or do you agree with the filmmaker's perspectives?

Social and political contexts

Look online at images and videos of the **Isle de Jean Charles, Southern Louisiana** where *Beasts of the Southern Wild* was filmed.

On YouTube, watch the CNN video report '98% of this Louisiana community has disappeared' and the short documentary *Last Stand on the Island* on how climate change has affected the area and its residents. Then answer the following questions:

Write an analysis of how *Beasts of the Southern Wild* represents Wink as a single father. Include:

- How the film deliberately avoids idealising parenthood, portraying Wink as a flawed character.
- The use of a non-actor (Dwight Henry).
- How spectators are positioned in relation to Wink – do you feel conflicted towards him?

A key influence on *Beasts of the Southern Wild* was the documentary *Dry Wood* (Blank, 1973). Watch extracts from the documentary and note down the similarities with *Beasts*.

Search online for **WJEC Eduqas Study Guide:** *Spectatorship and Ideology in* Beasts of the Southern Wild. Complete the activities contained in the study guide.

1. What has caused the flooding in Isle de Jean Charles?
2. How have climate change and industry affected the geography and people who live there?
3. How do local people feel about what is happening to their community? Why are they so keen to stay?
4. What similarities are there between the news report, the documentary and *Beasts*?

Activity

Social, historical and political contexts

Watch footage of Hurricane Katrina and New Orleans from news media reports available on YouTube and in documentaries.

- Create a poster explaining what happened. Include maps of the area, images of the storm from news media and information about the damage of the storm. Also include criticisms of the lack of a quick response from President George Bush.
- Write a 400-word analysis of how *Beasts of the Southern Wild* can be read as a comment on the impact of Hurricane Katrina.

Activity

Institutional contexts

Beasts of the Southern Wild was produced by the independent production company Court 13. According to Zeitlin, '*At Court 13, we're attempting to create art within our own system by our own special code. We want to keep the family intact, generate original material and tell our own stories.*'

Watch the Fox Searchlight *Beasts of the Southern Wild* Featurette: Court 13 on YouTube. Look at the Court 13 website https://court13arts.org

Write a short report on Court 13. Include:

- Who are Court 13?
- What are the aims and mission of Court 13?
- What type of films do they produce?
- How do Court 13 gain funding?
- How do the structure and working practices of Court 13 compare to larger studio production?
- What were their approaches to producing *Beasts of the Southern Wild*?

Key sequence analysis: the storm and its aftermath

Write a 400-word analysis of the sequences where Hushpuppy and Wink deal with the storm, then the following sequence which shows the devastation of the storm. Focus on the **core and specialist areas**. Use the following questions to help structure your analysis.

- How do elements of film form represent the storm from the perspective of Hushpuppy? Think about how filmic devices are used to align us with Hushpuppy during the storm and create a sense of fear, uncertainty and claustrophobia.
- How does the aftermath of the storm contrast with the storm itself? Think about how elements of film form, such as editing, cinematography and sound, are used differently in both sequences.
- How do the aftermath scenes compare to actual aerial footage of the aftermath of Katrina? Look at news footage of Katrina online to help you compare.

Revision activity

Spectatorship and *Beasts of the Southern Wild*

Answer the following short essay question:

How does the film align us with Hushpuppy by deliberately not explaining everything to us (e.g. Wink's illness)? Give examples from the film.

Revision activity

Read the sample annotated response on *Beasts of the Southern Wild* on page 159 of the textbook. Turn it into a 40-mark response by writing an extra paragraph using a different key sequence from the film.

Captain Fantastic (Ross, 2016)

Revising the core areas of film form and aesthetics in *Captain Fantastic*

Activity

Re-watch the **opening sequences** and the **church/funeral sequence** of *Captain Fantastic*. Write an analysis of the sequences, focusing on film form and aesthetics. Use the following questions to help structure your analysis.

The opening sequences

- How are editing and cinematography used to position us with the hunted deer?
- How are costume and make-up used to initially distance us from the Cash family during the hunting scenes?
- How are mise-en-scène, cinematography and sound used to humanise the Cash family after the hunt? Think about the use of props such as the family photograph.
- How are filmic devices used to show the Cash's affinity with nature?
- How would you describe the overall aesthetic of the opening sequences? How does this convey the themes and issues explored in the film?

The church/funeral sequence

Revision activity

Most of *Captain Fantastic* was shot in western Washington. Look at images of the area and search for interviews with the location scout Dave Drummond.

Create a poster with annotated stills of the film, explaining why this area was chosen and what it adds to the film's overall aesthetic.

Revision activity

Read pages 59–62 of the textbook on representations of age in *Captain Fantastic*.

Highlight the key points to help you revise representations.

- How is costume used to emphasise binary oppositions?
- How does this traditional Christian funeral contrast with the cremation service towards the end of the film?
- How are filmic devices used to portray the funeral as stuffy and traditional?
- How are filmic devices used in the scene outside the church to elicit sympathy with the grandparents?

Activity

Film form and aesthetics

Read this extract from an interview with director Matt Ross where he explains why he chose to shoot *Captain Fantastic* handheld:

'One of the things decided very early on was that we were going to shoot handheld. Originally, we had decided as the film got into the so-called "real world" it was going to become increasingly locked off. We were going to put the camera on the tripod more and it was going to become rigid like the world was rigid. But we found that was a formal idea that didn't really bear fruit. It's a nice idea but when we started doing it, it wasn't working for me emotionally ... I wanted to shoot handheld because ... I felt a more classical or formal manifestation of photography would put you at an arm's length. I wanted to be in the scene, not watch the scene.'

Answer the following questions:

- Do you agree that shooting handheld makes you feel like you are 'in' the scene? Give reasons for your answer.
- Give examples from the films where handheld is used effectively to add an intensity to the sequence.

Activity

Aesthetics and ideology

Create a poster, using annotated images from the film, which conveys the following conflicting lifestyles and ideologies visually:

- Freedom vs conformity
- Nature vs modernity
- Communist values vs capitalist values.

Explain how the aesthetics are achieved through mise-en-scène, lighting and cinematography.

Activity

Representations of age and gender

We will focus on the two Cash children who go through a change during the film. Consider Rellian Cash's rebellion against his father's beliefs and lifestyle and Bodevan Cash's 'coming of age' journey.

In the table on the following page, write bullet points on how each of these characters are represented in the film. Choose two key sequences for each character which feature the characters rebelling or transforming (e.g. the sequence where Bodevan meets Claire). Consider how the characters are represented in those sequences and how we as spectators may be aligned or distanced from them.

Character	Key sequences	Representations of age and gender
Rellian Cash		
Bodevan 'Bo' Cash		

Activity

Representations of gender

Look at the following statements on the representations of gender in *Captain Fantastic*:

- 'It is only the male characters who go on a journey and transformation in *Captain Fantastic*. The female characters are not explored in the same depth.'
- '*Captain Fantastic* is progressive in its representation of gender equality.'

Write a short argument for and against each of these statements. Use examples from the film as evidence for your arguments.

State which feminist ideological viewpoint on the film you most agree with and why.

Activity

Institutional contexts

Read this extract from an interview with director Matt Ross on independent film:

'Digital technology has democratised the means of production, and to a degree, distribution as well. Making films has perhaps never been easier; excellent cameras are available and inexpensive. Independent film in the US is vibrant and thriving. Getting people to find and watch your films, however, is still difficult. The major studios in the US are primarily in the business of making spectacles for global audiences, though there are exceptions, of course. Honestly, the studio world is not one I know well, so I can't speak with an insider's perspective. Excellent films are still made within that model, but it appears to be harder and harder to make certain kinds of films there. But I think as long as filmmakers make films, there will be audiences who want to see them.'

Use this quotation and your own knowledge of independent cinema and *Captain Fantastic* to answer the following questions:

- What are some of the main difficulties for independent producers in getting films distributed and exhibited?
- Ross states that independent film is thriving. The year 2014 (when *Captain Fantastic* was released) was a golden one for indie cinema. Find out the top grossing indie films of 2014. Why do you think there are so many critically acclaimed indie films? Think about audience tastes and the market for indie cinema.
- What are the benefits of distributing indie films for subsidiaries of major studios such as Fox Searchlight and Sony Pictures Classics?

Revision activity

Matt Ross has stated that non-US audiences responded differently to *Captain Fantastic* from US audiences. He noticed that French and UK audiences were more vocal about the film's criticisms of the USA.

Search for US and non-US critical responses to the film.

Note down the differences between responses. Why do you think that non-US critics responded to the film differently?

Representations of political contexts and ideology

Ben and Jack (Grandpa) have two different approaches to life. However, both are portrayed sympathetically, and both want the best for their family.

List the core political and personal beliefs of Ben and Jack, with examples from the film. Give arguments both for and against their beliefs as suggested in the film. The first example is started for you.

Character	Core beliefs	For	Against
Ben	1. Home-schools his children. Does not believe in formal education.	Ben's children are far more knowledgeable than his sister's children as evidenced in the 'Bill of Rights' scene.	Bodevan informs Ben that all his knowledge comes from books but he actually knows very little. Ben compromises at the end as his children wait for the school bus.
Character	Core beliefs	For	Against
Jack			

Key sequence analysis: the family dinner and the Bill of Rights

Write or record an audio commentary for the sequences where Ben and the children have dinner with Harper's family (including the argument in the garden outside) and the sequence where Ben asks Harper's children to explain the Bill of Rights. Focus on spectatorship and ideology, using the questions below to help structure your commentary.

The dinner sequence

- Do you agree with Ben's approach to parenting or do you think his actions, such as giving the children wine, are inappropriate? Think about how the scene is constructed to allow the spectator to respond in differing ways.
- How does the dinner scene challenge our own assumptions about family rules and rituals?

- How is humour derived from the **juxtapositions** between family members?
- When Ben and his sister and husband argue in the garden, how are filmic devices used to allow you to view both perspectives?

The Bill of Rights sequence

- What comment does this sequence make about the schooling system in America?
- What is the dominant reading of this sequence? What would a negotiated and oppositional reading be?
- Compare this sequence to the sequence where Bodevan tells his father he wants to go to college, arguing that 'Unless it comes out of a book I don't know anything'. How does this sequence offer a different perspective on home schooling?

Sample essay on visuals, sound and spectatorship in *La La Land* and *Beasts of the Southern Wild*

This sample uses extracts from WJEC Eduqas exemplar materials

My two films, *La La Land* and *Beasts of the Southern Wild* have much to offer in terms of visual and soundtrack cues, resulting in the spectator's response being influenced in a variety of ways. It could be argued that the viewer could quite easily become immersed in the escapist visuals used in the film *La La Land*.

In the spectacular opening sequence of *La La Land* establishing Chazelle's aesthetic of fantasy, it is an immediately immersive single take that resonates the style of Musicals from the Golden Age. It is an advert for the hope that LA represents: *La La Land* is a magical place where dreams are made and broken. The one-take opening scene uses grand cinematography, the crane shot swings out to an epic wide shot during the last note of the spectacle, showing us the most important character in the film: LA itself. The colour used in *La La* is a story, the vibrant colour palette is established, using primary colours, optimistic yellows, creative blues and passionate reds. In the opening scene, these colours are separate; the lack of connection between these bold colours tells us a bit about Hollywood, it is all about perfection. The use of colour in this way is a symbol of Hollywood, especially the Golden era musicals it emulates, but using this primary tri-colour palette makes it feel contemporary too. The colours feel separate and unconnected in the beginning, but start to blend and become warm as the narrative progresses and, as Mia and Sebs' love grows, more warm and romantic purples are added to the palette in the famous tap-dancing scene, for example, to connote that the characters and their associated colours have become connected. This is stripped away as their relationship breaks down and the singular primary colours start to be introduced.

Detailed analysis of a key sequence

The scene where Seb misses Mia's show demonstrates an interesting use of visuals to manipulate spectator response, Mia's show is a disaster, the mise-en-scène reflects this. The theatre is cold and grey, low-key, low-contrast light connotes Mia's sadness; this is her lowest point, which is juxtaposed by cross-cutting to Seb's Hollywood photoshoot, Chazelle uses the tri-colour palette here, but the colours are not blended and soft, they are separate and disconnected, which connotes the falseness of fame and Hollywood. In the opening sequence the traffic jam is symbolic of modern life, the feeling of being stuck, that society is stagnated, implying that this will not be a traditional love story. All the performers in the opening sequence imply that they have big dreams, like Mia and Seb, the bittersweet connotations are that Mia and Seb are not a special love story, they are an everyday one, they are just one of those Los Angeleans, one story in the crowd fighting to be heard. The soundtrack in the opening scene echoes this bittersweet idea, the lyrics

Detailed analysis discussing spectator alignment

of the opening number tell us of sacrifice and loss, which is hidden by the glamourous spectacle of LA life.

Detailed filmic references

In *Beasts of the Southern Wild* visual and soundtrack cues are used to align us with Hushpuppy and view the world from her perspective. Mise-en-scène and sound prove to be a powerful way of bringing the spectator closer to the natural world that Hushpuppy and her community love, respect and embrace. We see the wild and almost primitive way the people of the Bathtub live, for example the school room, which is a cabin set adrift the water, or the insects and farm animals that are captured as part of the environment the community cherishes. A spectator who sees Hushpuppy's father throw a whole chicken onto the fire for dinner, sees the close-up of her when she attends to a bird in its nest or sees and hears the flies buzzing around, may come to the conclusion that the Bathtub, whilst being her father's choice, is not ideal for her. The use of Hushpuppy's voice-over throughout the film further encourages the spectator to see the world through the eyes of a child. In the opening sequences, Hushpuppy describes the Bathtub as 'the prettiest place in the world', while the 'dry world' is show in long shot – a world of ugly pylons, creating a distance between us and the world the spectator would be familiar with.

Understanding of the film's themes and messages

Spectator alignment

In an early sequence, when her dad is taken to hospital unexpectedly, the mise-en-scène of the hut effectively invites the spectator to see Hushpuppy's loneliness, as she tries to cook dinner. Meanwhile, this mise-en-scène captures her longing for her absent mother, as we see that Hushpuppy has created a mum by piecing together her belongings, including a necklace and garments, with her own drawing. This sequence invites the spectator to feel sympathy for Hushpuppy, who needs her mother's tenderness. Therefore, it encourages the spectator to appreciate how Hushpuppy frequently addresses the spectator, creating an intimacy with them so she can share her feelings.

Overall, visual and soundtrack cues are used to encourage a particular response through aligning us with Mia in *La La Land* and Hushpuppy in *Beasts of the Southern Wild*.

Finish it

Complete the following practice 40-mark exam question response on American film using *Carol* and *Captain Fantastic*. The first short paragraph is written for you. Refer to two key sequences from each of the American films you have studied.

Explore how spectators may respond differently to the same character in the American films you have studied.

Spectators may respond differently to the same character due to their differing political beliefs. However, we should also consider that a film will be constructed to align us with characters who we can feel empathy towards regardless of our different beliefs.

British film since 1995 (two-film study)

What to revise

The core areas:

- **Film form**: cinematography, mise-en-scène, sound, editing and performance
- **Representations** and **aesthetics**
- Social, cultural, political, historical and institutional (including production) **contexts**.

The specialist areas:

- **Narrative**
- **Ideology.**

How you will be assessed at A Level

- In the examination, you will choose one question out of a choice of two.
- The question is worth **40 marks**.
- You are assessed on your knowledge and understanding of the two British films you have studied.
- You could be asked a question about the specialist areas of narrative and ideology.

How to approach a 40-mark question on British film

- We recommend that you spend 50 minutes maximum answering the question (including planning time).
- You do not need to compare the films.
- Link the specialist areas of narrative and ideology to your close analysis of the films.
- You are not expected to know or name-drop theorists' names (if you have been taught them).
- You do not need to describe or explain any theories related to spectatorship and ideology. Focus on applying them to the film.

AS Level

What to revise

The core areas:

- **Film form**: cinematography, mise-en-scène, sound and editing
- **Representations** and **aesthetics**
- Social, cultural, political, historical and institutional (including production) **contexts**.

The specialist areas:

- **Narrative** (including critical approaches).

How you will be assessed at AS Level

- In the examination, you will answer two questions. Question 1a is worth **20 marks**, then you will choose **either** question 1b **or** 1c, which are worth **40 marks**.
- You are assessed on your knowledge and understanding of the two British films you have studied.
- You could be asked a question about the specialist area of narrative.

Knowledge booster

Formalism refers to the distinction between **story** and **plot**.

Structuralism refers to how the narrative is structured to convey the plot, themes and messages. Examples include **binary oppositions, linear narrative**, and **open and closed endings.**

Activity

Provide definitions for all the key terms above in bold.

Revising specialist areas

Narrative

The specification states that you should study the following aspects of narrative:

- How the narrative is constructed through elements of film form.
- The use of **narrative devices**, including voice-over, flashback and repetition.
- How the narrative provides psychological insights into a character.
- Ambiguity – e.g. how we may not easily identify with certain characters.
- How the film is constructed to align the spectator with a particular character.
- What elements of film form the filmmakers select and how they combine them to create meaning.
- How the narrative and characters may be typical or atypical of the film's genre.

Critical approaches to narrative:

- The **distinction between story and plot**.
- **Binary oppositions**.
- How the narrative conveys **messages** and **values**.

Ideology

The specification states that you should study the following:

- The connotations of visual elements and sounds.
- Binary oppositions, e.g. good vs evil.
- How spectators are positioned and addressed.
- Ideological approaches (such as a feminist or a political perspective).
- An evaluation of the **ideological critical approach** to film.

Activity

Evaluating critical approaches

When evaluating critical approaches, you might consider how useful they have been for helping you understand the film in a way you had not previously considered.

Answer these questions for each of the British films you have studied to help you evaluate ideological critical approaches:

- Identify your own position on the film – what was your ideological response to the film?
- Think about the reasoning behind your response. Your own reaction to a film is an ideological standpoint. What are your own ideological views?
- Identify an opposing ideology – what is another way of looking at the film?
- Describe the reasoning behind the opposing ideology – why might someone else hold a different ideological response to the film?
- What does the different approach reveal about the film?
- What does the approach not reveal about the film? What other approaches may be used?
- Summarise what you have learned about how the film may elicit different ideological responses.

Practice essay question on British film

How far do the opening sequences of the British films you have studied reinforce ideological messages?

- Set a timer for 50 minutes to practise exam timings.
- Refer to at least one key sequence from each British film you have studied.
- Look at the mark scheme in the WJEC Eduqas Specimen Assessment Materials (online) and and assess your own work.
- Consider swapping essays with a fellow student and marking each other's response.

Revision tip

You should be able to evaluate the **critical approaches** of narrative and ideology in relation to the films you have studied. Critical approaches are ways of studying film that may help you to evaluate and reflect on the films – e.g. if you are studying a film from a feminist perspective, you may reflect on how women are represented in the film.

You may think about how you can compare and contrast different critical approaches to the film – e.g. how does a Marxist approach to the film offer different insights than a feminist approach to the film? Ask yourself: *How useful are critical approaches to narrative and ideology for understanding the films you have studied?*

Trainspotting (Boyle, 1996)

"HOLLYWOOD COME IN ...YOUR TIME IS UP
TRAINSPOTTING IS HERE AND IT'S TOE-CURLINGLY GOOD" ★★★★★
EMPIRE

#1 BEGBIE #2 DIANE #3 SICK BOY #4 SPUD #5 RENTON

Activity
Aesthetics

Create a poster on the aesthetics of *Trainspotting*. Research the following terms and provide definitions and examples of each aesthetic from *Trainspotting* on your poster:

- Magic realism
- Hyperrealism
- Expressionist use of light and colour.

Representations of gender, age and ethnicity in *Trainspotting*

Activity
Representations of age

Research the characteristics of Generation X and youth culture of the late 1980s and early 1990s.

Create a poster titled 'Generation X and *Trainspotting*'.

Include your research, annotated stills from the film and the following quotations:

- Director Danny Boyle: '*We wanted to make an exciting film ... a film about youth.*'
- Author of *Britpop Cinema*, Matt Glasby: '*A heroin film made by (and certainly for) the Ecstasy generation.*'

Activity
Representations of gender

Re-watch the sequences where Renton meets Diane and stays overnight at her parents' home. Write or record an audio commentary on the representations of gender in the sequences. Include:

- The use of the male gaze when Renton first meets Diane.
- How Diane is then represented as not simply a passive object of the male gaze.
- How Diane is much younger than Renton yet is mature for her age.

Revision activity

Search on YouTube for the video 'How *Trainspotting* became the voice of a generation'.

Answer the following questions:

1. What does the film's title *Trainspotting* mean?

2. What does the 'Choose Life' monologue mean?

3. The video states that *Trainspotting* is a film about transitions. What are some of the main transitions?

Representations of ethnicity

Re-watch the sequence where Renton speaks about how Scottish people are perceived as 'the lowest of the low'. Use Renton's speech and other examples from the film to write a short 500-word essay on how white working-class Scottish people are represented in *Trainspotting*.

Revision activity

Create a poster showing all the intertextual references to popular culture in *Trainspotting*. Include Sick Boy's love of James Bond films and the characters mimicking The Beatles' *Abbey Road* album cover.

Revising the contexts of *Trainspotting*

Cultural and institutional contexts

Read this introduction by Matt Glasby from his book *Britpop Cinema* (2019):

> 'In the mid-1990s, something strange happened to British cinema. People actually started to watch it. Beginning with Danny Boyle, John Hodge and Andrew Macdonald's Shallow Grave *(Boyle, 1995)*, going global with the same team's Trainspotting *(Boyle, 1996)*, and encompassing hits as diverse as Lock, Stock and Two Smoking Barrels *(Ritchie, 1998)*, Human Traffic *(Kerrigan, 1999)*, Billy Elliot *(Daldry, 2000)*, Sexy Beast *(Glazer, 2001)*, 24 Hour Party People *(Winterbottom, 2002)*, Shaun of the Dead *(Wright, 2004)*, The Football Factory *(Love, 2004)* and This is England *(Meadows, 2007)*, a genre I call 'Britpop Cinema' sprang up. It pushed boundaries, paid Hollywood little heed and, all too briefly, placed a booming UK film industry at the centre of its own movie universe.'

Glasby also notes that 128 British films were produced in 1996, compared with 30 in 1989.

Create a PowerPoint presentation titled 'The rise of British cinema in the late 1990s/ early 2000s'. Explain how and why this rise occurred.

Include slides on the following:

- The importance of policy decisions from organisations such as the New Labour Government (1997–2010), National Lottery, the BFI, Channel 4 for funding and nurturing British films. (There are plenty of articles and policy documents online for you to research this area. Search for 'New Labour and film policy'.)
- How and why these British films differed from the social realist films usually associated with British cinema.
- How these films were promoted. Search for posters and trailers for some of the films Glasby mentions.
- How these films contributed to and captured the zeitgeist of 'cool Britannia' and the rise of Britpop.
- The importance of *Trainspotting*'s commercial and critical success.

Social and historical contexts

Research the **HIV and AIDS epidemic** of the 1980s. Search online for poster campaigns, archive newspaper reports and television news articles and documentaries.

Write a 500-word essay on how *Trainspotting* represents the HIV virus and AIDS. Include:

- How *Trainspotting* reflects the hostility and misunderstanding towards people diagnosed with HIV or AIDS.
- Examples in *Trainspotting* where HIV and AIDS are explained and discussed by characters.
- How representations of HIV and AIDS in *Trainspotting* compare with news and documentary footage of the 1980s. (If you search for 'HIV AIDS 1980s' on YouTube you will find lots of examples of archive news footage.)

Political and historical contexts

Read the following statements from author Irvine Welsh on *Trainspotting*'s political contexts:

'*They were people in a transition, who got the shitty stick of de-industrialisation, but still had their humanity and were trying to get on and do something. I saw the heroin as basically just something people were doing in the absence of anything else to give their lives compelling drama ... so I didn't see them as victims, that was really important....*'

'*By 1983 you had 3.6 million unemployed. It tells its own story – you've got a lot of people with a lot of time on their hands. The government was basically creating demand. And they were naive. You're talking about people who wouldn't normally be involved in the heroin scene.*'

Provide a brief summary of each of the following factors that led to the rise of heroin addiction as explored in the film. (You can search online for relevant articles and documentaries.) Give examples from the film of how the following factors are represented and explored:

Revision activity

Trainspotting had a prolific and iconic marketing campaign. Search online for the posters used to promote the film.

Answer the following questions:

1. How do the posters capture the zeitgeist of 'cool Britannia'?

2. What is distinct and interesting about the posters in comparison to posters for mainstream films?

Revision activity:

Research 1990s 'New Lad' culture. Answer the following question:

What was New Lad Culture of the 1990s and how does *Trainspotting* reflect and represent this culture?

Key factors / Issues	Examples and representations in *Trainspotting*
De-industrialisation	
High unemployment	
The influx of cheap heroin in Scotland	

Activity

Social contexts and Ideology

Revision activity

Re-watch the sequence in *Trainspotting* where the main characters go out to a nightclub and Renton first meets Diane.

Write a 500-word analysis of how sound is used in this sequence. Include:

- The use of subtitles to add realism and humour.
- Sound – the nightclub scene.
- The importance of the soundtrack, including how Sleeper's cover of Blondie's 'Atomic' creates a nostalgic but contemporary vibe.

Read the following two opposing statements on *Trainspotting*:

- '*Trainspotting* glorifies heroin addiction and wraps it up in a cool, Britpop package.'
- '*Trainspotting* uses elements of fantasy and **surrealism** to show the grimness and desperation of heroin addiction. It de-glamorises drug use.'

Write down points for and against each argument, with examples from the film. Then indicate which statement you most agree with and why.

Activity

Contexts and Ideology

Re-watch the sequences where Renton moves to London, and Begbie comes to stay with Renton. Write or record an audio commentary for the sequence, focusing on contexts and ideology. Use the following bullet points to help structure your commentary.

- How London is initially represented as an exciting place to live.
- The representation of the London property boom of the 1990s.
- The rich/poor divide in London – e.g. Renton's run-down flat and the lyrics to Pulp's 'Mile End'.
- Representations of 1990s Rave culture.
- Representations of gender and sexuality – London as a more sexually liberal place.

Revising the specialist area of narrative in *Trainspotting*

Re-watch the sequence where Begbie throws the pint glass off the balcony and both Begbie and Renton recount what happened next. Answer the following questions:

- How is Renton's voice-over used to move the story back and forth in time?
- Do you think Renton's version of events is more reliable than Begbie's? Give reasons for your answer.
- How are other characters' versions of events mediated through Renton (e.g. Renton stating that he got 'the truth from Tony')?
- What is the impact of shifting from Begbie's to Renton's perspective?
- How is the shift in narration depicted through filmic devices (e.g. the freeze-frame)?

Revision activity

Watch '*Trainspotting* is 20' on the Kermode Uncut YouTube channel. Make notes on why the film is so iconic.

Revision activity

Search online for the *Trainspotting* screenplay. Choose one sequence from the screenplay and film. Write a short 400-word essay on how performance in the film gives meaning not found in the screenplay.

Key sequence analysis: the opening and closing sequence

Compare the opening and end sequences of *Trainspotting*. Using bullet points, answer the following questions:

- How does the opening monologue and title sequence contrast with the next scene at Mother Superior's?
- What do we learn about the main characters through the freeze-frames? Consider performance, costume and cinematography.
- What is the impact of beginning with a sequence that is mid-way through the plot? Think about how the plot is presented to us.
- Consider Renton's voice-over from an anti-capitalist, ideological perspective. How and why does he reject the capitalist lifestyle?
- What is your own reaction to the 'choose life' speech? Did it encourage you to critique capitalist lifestyles?
- Compare and contrast the opening sequences. How are binary oppositions used?
- How has Renton embraced a capitalist, individualistic lifestyle?
- How do you respond to the ending? Do you agree with Renton's choice or do you think the filmmakers encourage us to view Renton's new lifestyle in a critical way?

Sightseers (Wheatley, 2012)

Revising the core areas of *Sightseers*

Search on YouTube for the video essay

'Sightseers: Creativity in a Caravan'.

Watch the video and answer the following questions:

1. How is power and ownership conveyed in the film?

2. How are landscapes used in symbolic ways?

3. What references does the film make to Paganism and witchcraft?

Search online for 'WJEC EDUQAS Approaches to studying Sightseers'. Download the resource and complete the activities in the student guide.

Activity
Aesthetics

Create a poster on the aesthetics of *Sightseers*. Annotate stills from the film. Include:

- How landscape shots are used to emphasise humour and mood.
- Juxtapositions between the mundanity of aspects of British life and extreme violence.
- The use of surreal juxtapositions – e.g. the giant pencil.

Representations of age, gender and ethnicity

Complete the table below commenting on the representations of the key characters in *Sightseers*. Give examples from the film.

Key character	How key character is represented	Examples from the film
Tina	*Immature and infantile* *Becomes more independent*	
Chris	*Controlling* *Psychotic*	
Tina's mother	*Stereotype of bitter, lonely old woman*	

Cultural and institutional contexts

Director Ben Wheatley and writer Amy Jump's films are examples of **New British Realism**. This refers to contemporary British auteurs, including Andrea Arnold and Shane Meadows, who make more poetic and cinematic British realist films than traditional realist auteurs Ken Loach and Mike Leigh.

Wheatley and Jump's films combine social realism, macabre black comedy and genre films. BBC Entertainment reporter Tim Masters describes their films as '*black comedy and extreme violence splashed liberally across a distinctively British canvas*'.

Watch extracts from their previous films *Down Terrace* (2009) and *Kill List* (2011). Complete the **Venn diagram** to demonstrate the overlap and differences between more traditional British realist films and Ben Wheatley's New British Realism.

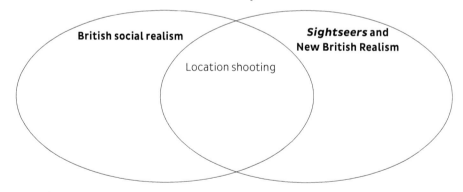

British social realism

Sightseers and New British Realism

Location shooting

Revision activity

Alice Lowe and Steve Oram created the comic characters of Tina and Chris through improvisation and taking a caravanning holiday together in character. Write a short 400-word essay on how improvisation adds to the performance and impact of the film.

Institutional contexts

Read the following extract from Wendy Mitchell on ScreenDaily.com (2012):

> '*They (Alice Lowe and Steve Oram) pitched a* Sightseers-*like TV series that didn't get off the ground, but through that pitch they got noticed by director Edgar Wright, who introduced the pair to his usual production company, Big Talk (Wright executive produces).*
>
> *Such collaboration and encouragement for new voices should be commended – and a "well done" for Big Talk seeing the promise in Lowe and Oram's story and developing the project for years.*'

Look at the website bigtalkproductions.com and answer the following questions:

- Which film genres do Big Talk Productions specialise in?
- How do the company describe themselves and their ethos?
- How does *Sightseers* fit into the company's USP and ethos?

Revising the specialist areas of narrative and ideology in *Sightseers*

Binary oppositions

Give examples of the following binary oppositions in *Sightseers*, then state the impact of the oppositions – e.g. to create dramatic tension:

Binary opposition examples in *Sightseers*	Impact of the binary oppositions
Social class: working class vs middle class	
The mundane and the macabre	
Realism and surrealism	
Comedy and horror	
Restrictions vs freedom	
The urban and the rural	

Narrative and genre

1. Create a knowledge organiser explaining the conventions of the following film genres used in *Sightseers*. Look for examples of knowledge organisers online if you are unfamiliar with them.
   - Horror
   - Comedy
   - The Road Movie
   - British Social Realism.

Revision activity

Film critic Mark Kermode notes that *'as they (Chris and Tina) get further and further away from the rules of acceptable behaviour, they go off into more and more remote and cinematic landscapes'*.

Create a flowchart poster of Tina and Chris' journey in chronological order. Provide annotated stills of each place they visit to demonstrate how the landscapes become more remote.

For each genre, include:

- Definitions of the genre, including a brief history
- Narrative conventions
- Common character types
- Key influential films.

2. Write a 500-word essay on how *Sightseers* uses and subverts elements of these genres. Give examples from the film in your response.

Activity
Ideological critical approaches

Apply the following three ideological critical approaches to *Sightseers*:

- **Marxism** – class divides
- **Feminism** – Tina's empowerment
- British identity and values – British codes of behaviour.

Create a PowerPoint presentation titled 'Applying three ideological approaches to *Sightseers*'. Include the following:

- An explanation of each approach.
- An application of each approach to *Sightseers* with examples from the film.
- Examples of how each approach offers us a different understanding and interpretation of the film.
- Points on the limitations of each approach.
- An explanation of the one or two approaches you found most useful for understanding the film and why.

Key sequence analysis: the opening and closing sequences

Re-watch the opening and closing sequences of *Sightseers*. Write a 1000-word comparison of the two sequences, focusing on the core and specialist areas. Use the bullet points and images below to help guide your analysis.

The opening sequences

- How themes, character and narrative are established in the opening sequence through the map, Tina's mother wailing and framed pictures of Poppy.
- The use of enigma – what happened to Poppy?
- How the relationship between Tina and her mother is established through visuals and sound.

Knowledge booster

Many critics noted that *Sightseers* reminded them of the Mike Leigh television play *Nuts in May* (1976). Read about *Nuts in May* and watch extracts, noting down the similarities between *Nuts in May* and *Sightseers*.

Revision activity

Read Adam's response to a question on *Trainspotting* and *Sightseers* on page 189 of the textbook. Turn it into a 40-mark response by adding more detail and referring to another key sequence from each film.

- How Tina's immaturity is conveyed, e.g. the use of the teddy bear.
- How the soundtrack 'Tainted Love' is used to comment on Tina's freedom from her mother and her relationship with Chris.

The closing sequences

- How imagery of the harsh desolate landscape contributes to the mood and conveys themes.
- The burning of the caravan as a symbol of freedom and destruction.
- Compare the setting in the final sequences to Tina's entrapment in her home in the opening sequences.
- Consider how the application of an ideological feminist approach can enable a reading of Tina as empowered by 'letting go' of Chris.
- Compare the use of 'Tainted Love' in the end credits with the Soft Cell version in the opening sequence – what is the significance of the upbeat, 1964 Motown version with a female singer (Gloria Jones)?

Sample essay on ideology and narrative in *Trainspotting* and *Sightseers*

This sample uses extracts from WJEC Eduqas exemplar materials.

The final scenes of a film allow the director to shape their concluding messages. *Trainspotting* and *Sightseers* offer the audience different perspectives on the world, *Trainspotting* was produced in a post-Thatcherite time and reflects of the negative effect of 'Tory' rule, while optimistically embracing the youthful 'Britpop' climate of empowerment. *Sightseers* is an example of New British Realism of the 21st century, combining social realism with a poetic use of location to comment on aspects of British life and culture.

Detailed analysis of the closing sequence

Powerful final sequences deliver a resolution that defines the director's 'final word' and this message is what the audience leave the cinema thinking about. *Trainspotting* offers the audience a generally restricted narrative through the character of Renton, we are introduced to his anti-establishment 'Manifesto' in the opening scene; in the final scene, however, Renton's 'Choose life' counter-cultural stance has flipped, he no longer wishes to reject dominant ideologies, he wants to be 'just like you' the 'us and them' binary opposition has shifted, he is now 'us'. Boyle's aesthetics during this voice-over contributes to the hopeful feeling he wants his audience to embrace. The halo-effect light of the dawn suggests a new era of enlightenment and presents Renton in a near angelic light; his 'clean' pale blue costume connotes an ironic innocence. In addition, this juxtaposes the sickly colours we associate with the aesthetic of addiction from previous scenes. Isolated locations have surrounded Renton from the start of the film (he is often shot apart from his mates, surrounded by negative space) and in the final moments this has been manipulated further; we see Renton in an extreme long-shot, he is a tiny spec in the deserted city, walking in the opposite direction to the traffic on a lonely bridge. This ending is not altogether hopeful; however, Renton's demonic grin and near breaking of the fourth wall feel like a challenge or threat to the audience. Yes, he has embraced the dominant capitalist ideology, but it has come at a price, he has swindled his friends; this is the cost of becoming a true capitalist consumer. Renton is literally walking into the sunrise, accompanied with a powerful energetic non-diegetic soundtrack; it is a new beginning.

The ending of *Sightseers* offers liberation for Tina, as she finally escapes the shackles of her controlling mother and boyfriend, Chris. When viewed through a feminist ideological lens, we can understand the message of the film as one of female empowerment. As Chris and Tina stand at the top of the viaduct, ready to leap to their deaths, Tina lets Chris' hand slip. Our attention is drawn to this important gesture through the use of slow motion as Tina deliberately lets his hand go. We then cut to a close-up of Tina's face as she has finally allowed herself to be free of him. The film can therefore be read as a redemptive journey for Tina, as it offers a deliberate binary opposition to the Tina we first meet in the beginning of the film, stood in the doorway of her Mother's home, desperately vying for her attention, followed by her need for approval from Chris. The use of the rugged but harsh natural landscape in the final sequences can be read as reflecting Tina's escape and the macabre nature of the film, as she too is a murderer. The long-shot of the burning of the caravan in the open countryside can be read as both the destruction of Tina and Chris' relationship but also Tina's decision to finally be free of Chris.

The non-diegetic soundtrack of 'Tainted Love' bookends the film. Through a feminist perspective we can understand the significance of this track to Tina's journey. When we hear it in the title sequences, it is the Soft Cell version of the song in a male voice, a comment on Chris and Tina's escape and 'tainted' relationship. The version used in the final credits is sung by a woman and now represents Tina's escape.

Both films offer the audience hope, an important part of the resolution phase of mainstream narratives (despite many counter-cultural elements within the ideological standpoint). *Trainspotting* allows the audience to consider that Renton is redeemed – (he shares some of his money with Spud, he 'doesn't give a shit' about Begbie and Sick Boy, 'they'd do the same to him' within this verisimilitude that rationale is acceptable), he is clean (which is reflected in the mise en scene) and he 'Chooses Life' according to his understanding of hegemony. Additionally, he is in London, the new 'swinging', Britpop, centre of Britain, he has 'escaped' 'shite' Scotland to live in London among the yuppie 'wankers'. *Sightseers* offers the audience a hope for Tina, the character the film most aligns us with and can be read as her journey. The final shot is the end of her character arc, a woman repressed by family (her mother) and patriarchy (Chris) who has finally broken free.

Finish it

Complete the following practice 40-mark exam question response on British film using *Trainspotting* and *Sightseers*. The first short paragraph is written for you. Refer to two key sequences from each of the British films you have studied.

How far do the narratives of British films you have studied use binary oppositions to create dramatic conflict?

Both *Trainspotting* and *Sightseers* use binary oppositions in complex ways to create drama but also convey messages and values. *Trainspotting* offers binary oppositions in lifestyles – the lifestyle of a heroin addict versus the 'choose life' mantra of a capitalist lifestyle. *Sightseers* offers binary oppositions of social class to create black humour and violent drama as the character Chris seeks revenge on often middle-class British holidaymakers who stand in his way.

Understanding of key messages through a political ideological approach

Detailed references to the final sequences

Application of a feminist approach

Understanding of narrative structure – use of binary oppositions

Global film (two-film study)

Knowledge booster

Other names for Global cinema include:

- World cinema
- Foreign-language cinema
- International cinema.

The Oscars often change the name for their Global film category. Search online to find out the various name changes for this category and state what your understanding is of these categories.

Revision activity

The films in the global film section are all examples of national cinemas or transnational co-productions.

For the two films you have studied, answer the following question:

To what extent do the two films you have studied appeal to national rather than international audiences?

What to revise

- The **core areas**: film form (cinematography, mise-en-scène, editing, sound and performance); representations (ethnicity, gender and age), aesthetics and contexts.

How you will be assessed at A Level

- You choose one essay question from a choice of two.
- The question is worth **40 marks**.

How to approach a 40-mark question on global film

- We recommend that you spend 60 minutes maximum answering the question, including planning.
- Refer to key sequences from the two films you have studied.
- You do not have to compare the two films.

AS Level

At AS Level: Section B: Non-English language European film

You have studied one non-English language European film.

What to revise

- The core areas: film form (cinematography, mise-en-scène, editing and sound); representations (ethnicity, gender and age), aesthetics and contexts.

How you will be assessed at AS Level

- You will answer two questions. Question 2a is worth **10 marks**. You will then choose either question 2b OR question 2c which is worth **20 marks**.
- We recommend you spend 10 minutes on question 2a and 20 minutes on question 2b OR 2c.

Practice question on global film

With close reference to the two films you have studied, explore how either performance or mise-en-scène create meaning.

- Set a timer for 60 minutes to practise exam timings.
- Refer to one or two key sequences from each film.
- Provide a short introduction and conclusion.
- Look at the assessment objectives and mark schemes in the Sample Assessment Materials (online) and assess your own work.
- Consider swapping essays with a fellow student and marking each other's response.

Pan's Labyrinth (Del Toro, Spain, 2006)

Case study 1

"DARK, TWISTED AND BEAUTIFUL...A MASTERPIECE"
★★★★

"EXQUISITE AND ENCHANTING. IT'S NOT TO BE MISSED"
★★★★

★★★★★   ★★★★★

Revising aesthetics and film form in *Pan's Labyrinth*

Activity

Aesthetics

Annotate the following images from *Pan's Labyrinth*, stating how they demonstrate the aesthetics of the film. Discuss how aesthetics are used to convey the film's themes and messages. Include:

- The aesthetics of fascism (e.g. Captain Vidal's world)
- The aesthetics of a gothic, violent fairy tale and references to well-known fairy tales and fables (e.g. the Pale Man)
- The aesthetics of womanhood and femininity (e.g. the uterus, fallopian tubes, circular doorways and caves)
- Pagan imagery (e.g. the ruins of the labyrinth)
- Catholic imagery (e.g. the Pale Man and the Pale Man's hall).

Revision activity

Search on YouTube for the video essay 'Pan's Labyrinth: Disobedient Fairy Tale'.

Make notes on the following, stating how areas of film form are used:

- How the film takes elements of the fairy tale and subverts them.
- Examples of characters' disobedience.
- Why the author thinks the fantasy elements are not in Ofelia's mind.

Image	Aesthetics
	*Womanhood. Image of a uterus.*
	Violent fairytale. Deep reds/oranges, danger.

Global film (two-film study): Case study 1   **85**

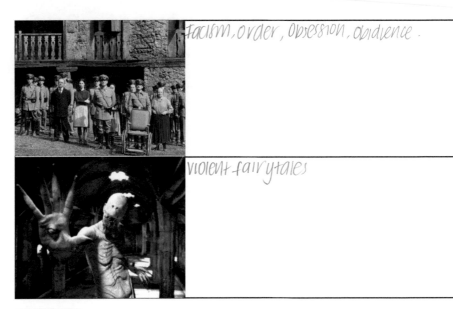

Facism, order, obsession, obidience.

violent fairytales

Knowledge booster

Del Toro was influenced by the paintings of Goya, particularly 'Saturn Devouring His Son'. The painting depicts the Greek myth that the Titan Cronus ate each one of his children upon their birth.

Note down the similarities between this painting and the Pale Man in *Pan's Labyrinth*.

Activity

The aestherics of fantasy and reality

Read the following statements:

- 'The fantasy sequences in *Pan's Labyrinth* are all in Ofelia's imagination. They are her coping mechanism for the harsh reality of life in post-civil war Spain.'
- 'Ofelia is not imagining the fantasy elements. The fantasy is just as harsh and violent as the reality.'

Write a justification for both statements using examples from the film. Then discuss which statement you find most convincing and why.

Activity

Themes and issues

For each theme or issue listed in the table below, give examples of how they are explored in *Pan's Labyrinth*. Refer to key moments or images in the film.

Theme/issue	Examples in *Pan's Labyrinth*
The abuse of power and how it affects people subjected to that power	
Time and the past	
The impact of war on children	
Self-sacrifice	

Revising representations and contexts in *Pan's Labyrinth*

Representations of masculinity: Captain Vidal

Write a short 500-word essay on how Captain Vidal embodies a toxic masculinity and the evils of fascism. Include:

- How Vidal's violence and aggressive masculinity is conveyed visually.
- How Del Toro links fascism ideology with hyper-masculinity.
- How Vidal's masculinity contrasts with femininity and female characters.
- How Vidal's death represents the destruction of fascism.
- The importance of patriarchal bloodlines to Vidal – Vidal's memories of his father and interest in his baby son.

Representations of age and femininity

Make notes on how Ofelia's and Mercedes's age and gender are represented in *Pan's Labyrinth*. Use the bullet points in the table to get you started.

Character	Representations of age and femininity
 Ofelia	- An independent child - Coming of age
Mercedes	- An example of a female anti-fascist - Role of protector and mother

Revision activity

Search on YouTube for the video 'The Pale Man (Pan's Labyrinth Explored)'.

Answer the following questions:

1. What was the Pale Man inspired by?

2. How is the Pale Man an **allegory** of Spain itself?

Historical and political contexts

Create a PowerPoint presentation explaining how *Pan's Labyrinth* reflects on Spain's past and also conveys the trauma and loss of innocence in a post 9/11 world. Use the BBC Bitesize online revision guide on the Spanish Civil War as a starting point. Include:

- Information about the Spanish Civil War and the Franco era.
- The impact of fascism and war on the ordinary people of Spain.
- How *Pan's Labyrinth* represents this era in Spanish history.
- The political, anti-fascist messages of the film.
- How the film reflects the impact of 9/11 on the world.

Cultural and institutional contexts

Answer the following questions on *Pan's Labyrinth* as a European film and its relationship to Hollywood cinema:

- Film academic José Arroyo described the film as '*a wonderful marriage of Hollywood genre and European art film*' (2006). Give examples of how the film combines genre film and art cinema.
- Del Toro has stated that a Hollywood studio would never make a film like *Pan's Labyrinth*. Give three reasons why a Hollywood studio may not make this film.

Revision activity

Cultural and institutional contexts

Pan's Labyrinth is the sister film to Del Toro's earlier film *The Devil's Backbone* (2001).

Watch extracts from *The Devil's Backbone* and give three examples of how *Pan's Labyrinth* is related to this film in terms of themes, genre and visual style.

Key sequence analysis: the final sequences

Write or record an audio commentary analysing the final sequences of *Pan's Labyrinth*, focusing on the core areas. Use the bullet points below to help structure your commentary.

- Visual representations of Vidal's loss of power.
- Colour juxtapositions – the use of blue and yellow.
- The use of cross-cutting to create tension.
- The use of non-diegetic music to heighten suspense and emotion.
- References to fairy tales – Ofelia's red cape and shoes.
- How camera movement reflects the circular imagery.
- How the final scenes reinforce messages and values.
- Representations of Mercedes and Ofelia as courageous and defying monsters.
- Mercedes as both a strong female freedom fighter and maternal, motherly figure.
- How the father's kingdom and male voice-over reinforce patriarchy.
- Symbolic imagery of Ofelia returning to the mother's womb.

Mustang (Ergüven, France/Turkey, 2015)

Revising aesthetics and film form in *Mustang*

Aesthetics

Read the following quotations about the aesthetics of *Mustang*:

Sophia Cowley, 'MUSTANG & Sister Solidarity in Modern-Day Turkey', Filminquiry.com (2016):

> 'The color palette in Mustang *is beautiful: blue, grey, and cool tones reflect rural calm. Since the girls are forced to spend most of their time indoors, they are often seen in relative darkness, the mood somber. But interspersed with these darker shots are playful, sun-lit moments. The light of day brings softer colors like light pink and seaside blue, which wash over the screen.*
>
> *At one point, the girls move from the dull, quiet countryside to an energetic red-toned soccer stadium. Brilliantly, the camera moves swiftly with them, in a hand-held style. The contrast between shots in the home and this new kind of movement is obvious and electric. Boredom meets excitement, the thrill of freedom captured in loud light and sound.'*

Director Deniz Gamze Ergüven:

> 'Aesthetically, what I was trying to do was to move away as much as possible from any form of naturalism … The architecture had something of Psycho and **German Expressionism**, something eerie and not-naturalistic. I was trying to move away from a potentially gloomy reality.'

Create a poster exploring the aesthetics of *Mustang*. Include the two quotations, with images from the film that demonstrate the points made in the quotes.

Revision activity

Answer the following questions on *Mustang*'s title:

1. Why is the film called *Mustang*?

2. Give examples of how the film's title relates to the representations of the girls in the film.

Knowledge booster quiz

1. Which three countries co-financed *Mustang*?

2. The film was the highest grossing Turkish film released in the UK. How much money did it make at the UK box office?

3. Whereabouts in Turkey was *Mustang* filmed?

Revision activity

Search online for 'Turkish Delight: A film scene with a rich history' on the BBC Culture website. Watch the short news report on Turkish cinema and answer the following question:

What new insights did you gain about the rich diversity of Turkish cinema?

Revision activity

Watch Mark Kermode's review of *Mustang* on YouTube.

Answer the following questions:

1. Which films provided the inspiration for Mustang?

2. What do Western critics such as Kermode find praiseworthy about the film?

Activity

Themes, issues and style

For each theme and issue, give examples of how *Mustang* conveys these through visuals and sound. Refer to key sequences or moments in the film.

Themes/issues	Examples
Freedom vs entrapment	
Rebellion	
Religious conservatism in rural Turkey	
Patriarchy	
Istanbul as a place of refuge	

Activity

Film form and realism

Write a short 500-word essay on how realism is created in *Mustang*. Use detailed examples from the film to illustrate your points. Include:

- The use of handheld shooting and observational cinematography.
- Non-professional actors.
- Location shooting.
- The use of real news footage on the television.
- The emotional impact of realist devices on the audience.

Revising the representations and contexts of *Mustang*

Activity

Historical, social and political contexts

Create a knowledge organiser describing Turkey, its population and politics. Include:

- Maps of the area, highlighting where Istanbul and rural Anatolia are located and information about these places.
- Information about Turkey's population, including the percentage of people who are Muslim.
- A brief summary of Turkey's recent history and politics.
- Information about the president of Turkey, Recep Tayyip Erdoğan. What are his beliefs, attitudes to women and economic reforms? How is he regarded in the West?

Gender, social, political and institutional contexts

Answer the following questions on gender and critical responses to *Mustang*:

- What do you learn about what it is like to be a teenage girl in rural Turkey through watching *Mustang*?
- Do you think *Mustang* is a feminist film? Does it relate to international feminist concerns, or do you think its concerns are nationally or regionally specific?

Read this extract from Alparslan Nas's *Media Representations of the Cultural Other in Turkey* (2018):

> 'In Turkey, Mustang *was released on October 23, 2015. It screened in only 16 theaters but was seen by 4046 viewers in the first three days of its release and by 25,419 viewers during its 22 weeks of screening, meeting with mixed responses from different Turkish film critics. While some authors celebrated the film for its feminist stance on male-dominated Anatolian culture, others critically discussed the film's narration of Anatolian conservatism and the Black Sea region, pointing out that the kinds of representation shown do not reflect the reality in such regions In particular, the film's portrayal of sisters in secularised outfits and showing secular behaviour did not reflect the reality of the local women, most of whom use the veil as part of their traditional clothing [...] representations are completely devoid of any Islamic signifiers, as if they were projected on the region from a Western society with a secularised imagery – which contradicts the religious culture dominating the villages in the Black Sea region.'*

The film was harshly criticised by the national critics for its **gendered orientalism**. This refers to a Western view of Eastern Muslim women as oppressed, powerless victims and Muslim men as barbaric and a threat that needs to be contained. Some local critics argued that because director Deniz Gamze Ergüven has lived between France and Turkey since she was two, she is 'not Turkish enough' and therefore projects a Western perspective onto rural Turkey.

- Do you agree that *Mustang* offers a 'gendered orientalism'? Make references to the representations of the girls and Uncle Erol. Use the extracts from Alparslan Nas's article to help develop your points.
- How has Ergüven responded to criticisms from Turkish critics? Search online for interviews with Ergüven about the film and read extracts from her interviews on pages 191-205 of the textbook.

Activity

Cultural contexts

Research **New Turkish Cinema** and create a PowerPoint exploring the contexts and characteristics of this movement in Turkish cinema. A good starting point for your research is the introduction in Asuman Suner's book *New Turkish Cinema: Belonging, Identity and Memory* (2010).

Include the following in your PowerPoint:

- The factors that led to New Turkish Cinema.
- The characteristics of New Turkish Cinema and how it differs from mainstream film.
- Key themes explored in New Turkish films, including the importance of national, social, religious, political and sexual identity.
- Examples of the diverse range of directors, including Nuri Bilge Ceylan and Zeki Demirkubuz.
- Importance of co-funding from European companies and success at European film festivals.
- A discussion of *Mustang* as an example of New Turkish Cinema – the similarities and differences between *Mustang* and other New Turkish films.

Revision activity

Representations of childhood in *Mustang*

Answer the following questions:

1. What did you learn about how girls under the age of 18 are treated in Turkey?

2. How do religious conservative views of childhood differ from Western ideals of childhood?

Key sequence analysis: the football match

Read this quote from Ergüven about the production of the sex scene in the car: *'The region where we were is extremely conservative. For example, the scene where Ece (Elit İşcan) has sex in the car in front of the bank, the production team completely panicked about that. The location manager was completely freaked out ... I was telling him "It's all right, we're just [being suggestive]," Nothing happened, but it was like, "Shoot your frame and run".'*

Answer the following questions:

1. Why might local people be upset by the shooting of this sequence?

2. What other juxtapositions are there in the film between the girls' want for freedom and the conservatism of the local area.

Re-watch the sequences where the girls decide to go to the football match, hitch a ride and attend the match. Write or record an audio commentary applying the core areas to the sequence. Use the bullet points below to help guide your commentary:

- How themes of freedom and imprisonment are portrayed through visuals and sound.
- The use of the handheld camera to convey urgency, energy and realism.
- Social and political contexts – a women-only audience for the football game.
- The use of cross-cutting to create tension between the girls at the match and the uncle at home.
- The sound of celebration and freedom on the bus and how this contrasts to the quiet, rural village.
- The use of slow motion and bright light to convey the girls' happiness at the match.

Key sequence analysis: the final sequences

Re-watch the final sequences of the film where Lale and Nur travel to Istanbul and arrive at their former teacher's apartment. Write or record an audio commentary applying the core areas to the sequence. Use the bullet points below to help guide your commentary:

- How the distance between the village and Istanbul is conveyed through cinematography, editing and mise-en-scène.
- The significance of the image of the bus driving through a dark tunnel into the light.
- How we see Istanbul through the eyes of Lale.
- Lale's memories of her childhood – how these are conveyed nostalgically through bright lighting.
- The use of close-ups of Lale to align the spectator with her.
- How Istanbul is represented as a place of refuge in opposition to the village.
- The difference in women's dress in Istanbul.
- The use of melancholic non-diegetic music.

Taxi Tehran (Panahi, Iran, 2015)

Revising the core areas of film form and aesthetics in *Taxi Tehran*

Aesthetics

Create a poster exploring the aesthetics of *Taxi Tehran*. Annotate images from the film to illustrate your points. Include examples of the following:

- Aesthetics of the everyday and ordinary people in Tehran.
- The Influence of documentary **cinéma vérité** and Italian neo-realism. (If you are unfamiliar with these film movements and styles, they are explained in the textbook on page 216.)
- Aesthetics of freedom and confinement.
- The taxi as a public and private space.
- The use of long takes and cameras inside the car.

Performance in Iranian films and *Taxi Tehran*

Iranian cinema is a **self-reflexive** cinema. There are many Iranian films which feature non-actors playing themselves or versions of themselves. A good example is the film *Close-up* (Kiarostami, 1990). The *New York Times* (online) describes *Close-up* as follows:

> Close-up *follows the actual trial of Hossain Sabzian, a Tehran cinephile who ingratiated himself with the well-to-do Ahankhah family, claiming to be the filmmaker Mohsen Makhmalbaf and asking to use their home and family for his next movie. To supplement the real trial footage, Kiarostami convinced Sabzian, the Ahankhahs, Makhmalbaf and other key figures to re-enact scenes as themselves.*

This compares to how Panahi and human rights lawyer Nasrin Sotoudeh play themselves in *Taxi Tehran*.

Revision activity

> Write a 500-word essay on the following question:
>
> Iranian director Mania Akbari argues that Iranian cinema 'looks poor on the outside but it's rich inside'. How far is this true of *Taxi Tehran*?

Answer the following essay question on this performance style in some Iranian films:

- 'The use on non-actors and people playing versions of themselves in Iranian film enhances the realism of the performances.' With reference to *Taxi Tehran*, how far do you agree with this statement?

Revising representations of gender, age and ethnicity in *Taxi Tehran*

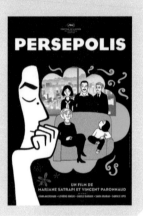
Activity

Representations of age

Compare the representations of the two older women with a goldfish with the child character Hanna. Make notes on the following:

- How the older women represent Iran's past through their superstitious attitude.
- How Hanna represents Iran's future as an independent young girl who wants to be a filmmaker.
- How the characters' views are shaped by Iranian culture and the political regime.

Activity

Representations of gender

Answer the following questions on representations of gender in *Taxi Tehran*:

- What do you know about how the patriarchal culture of Iran affects women?
- Did the representations of women in *Taxi Tehran* surprise you? Were the women more empowered than you expected? Give reasons and examples from the film.
- What did you learn about the issues facing some women from the stories recounted by human rights lawyer Nasrin Sotoudeh?

Activity

Representations of ethnicity and social and political contexts

Taxi Tehran features characters from a diverse cross-section of Iranian society, offering a microcosm of Iran's capital city Tehran.

For each of the following three passengers, make notes on how they represent an aspect of Iranian society. Include what you learn about Iranian society and politics from each passenger.

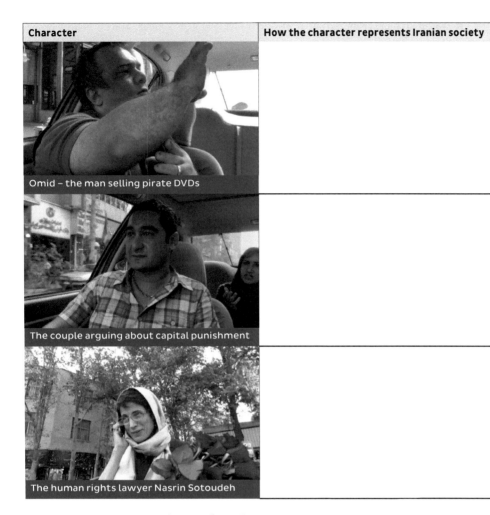

Character	How the character represents Iranian society
Omid – the man selling pirate DVDs	
The couple arguing about capital punishment	
The human rights lawyer Nasrin Sotoudeh	

The contexts of *Taxi Tehran*

Revision activity

Activity

Cultural contexts

Jafar Panahi worked as influential Iranian filmmaker Abbas Kiarostami's assistant and is heavily influenced by Kiarostami's films and approach to filmmaking. *Taxi Tehran* has been compared to Kiarostami's film *Ten* (2002), about a female driver and the conversations she has with ten different passengers.

Ten (Kiarostami, 2002)

Jafar Panahi was a supporter of the **Green Movement** in Iran. Research the Green Movement and the filmmakers involved in this movement. Answer the following questions:

1. What was the Green Movement and what were people involved in it protesting about?

2. What factors led to the rise of the movement?

3. How did the Iranian government respond to the protests?

4. How did involvement in the Green Movement affect filmmakers such as Jafar Panahi?

- Watch extracts from *Ten* and note down at least three comparisons between *Ten* and *Taxi Tehran*.

Comparisons:	Ten	Taxi Tehran
Visual style		
Themes and issues		
Structure		

Activity
Political contexts

Create a knowledge organiser about Iran's history, politics, culture and cinema. Include:

- A map of Iran with facts about its location, population, language and religion.
- Key facts about the 1979 Islamic revolution. Include what led to the revolution and how the revolution changed Iranian life and culture.
- How the politics of Iran has impacted on filmmakers who make films critiquing the regime.

Revision activity

On YouTube, watch the Vice Documentary 'Inside Iranian Cinema Parts 1, 2 and 3'. Make notes on what new insights you learn about Iranian cinema, its history and popularity in Iran and Europe.

Activity
Cultural, political and institutional contexts – the Iranian New Wave

Create a PowerPoint presentation titled 'Iranian **New Wave** cinema and *Taxi Tehran*'. Include clips from key Iranian films in your presentation slides.

Structure the slides as follows:

Slides 1–2: A brief history of Iranian cinema.

Slide 3: The importance of the film *The Cow* (Mehrjui, 1969).

Slides 4–5: A brief summary of the 1979 Islamic revolution and how it affected cinema.

Slide 6: The restrictions imposed on filmmakers after the revolution.

Slide 7: Key films and filmmakers of the Iranian New Wave beginning in the 1990s, including Abbas Kiarostami.

Slides 8–9: Characteristics of the Iranian New Wave, including allegory, realism and open endings.

Slide 10: The relationship between Europe and Iranian cinema – e.g. funding, festivals and distribution.

Slides 11–12: Application of New Wave characteristics and censorship and distribution issues to *Taxi Tehran* and Jafar Panahi.

Key sequence analysis: Hanna

Re-watch the sequences with Hanna in the taxi discussing filmmaking and her conversation with the young boy who she films.

Write or record an audio commentary analysing the core areas in this sequence. Use the bullet points below to help structure your commentary:

- What the sequence teaches us about how to make a distributable film in Iran.
- Representations of Hanna as a free-spirited, strong-willed girl.
- Point of view shots from Hanna's camera.
- How realism is created through location shooting, lack of non-diegetic sound and the cameras placed inside Panahi's car.
- How the scene comments on observational filmmaking as Hanna creates her own film of the wedding couple and the young boy.
- How Hanna reflects the prevalence of women directors in Iranian cinema.
- How the scene comments on the construction of narratives and defies conventional narratives – e.g. the young boy says, 'I don't want to be the hero'.

City of God (Mereilles, Brazil, 2002)

Revising film form and aesthetics in *City of God*

Activity
Aesthetics

Create a poster on the aesthetics of *City of God*. Annotate stills from each section of the film to show the changes in aesthetics as time passes. State in your annotations how aesthetics conveys the messages and themes of the film. Include:

- The changes in colour tone to reflect the changes in the favelas over time.
- The aesthetics of nostalgia and childhood in the first section of the film.
- The aesthetics of violence and brutality in the final section of the film.
- More night-time sequences during the scenes set in the early 1980s.
- MTV-style aesthetics (search online for the essay 'Pop, Speed and the "MTV Aesthetic" in Recent Teen Films' by Kay Dickinson if you are unsure what this means) – use of jump-cuts, rapid editing, freeze-frames and montage.

Activity
Film form in the opening sequences

Re-watch the opening sequences of *City of God*. Analyse the use of film form in the opening sequences. Make detailed revision notes using the bullet points below as a guide:

- The significance of the chicken.
- The use of rhythmic editing.
- How the key themes are established through visuals and sound.
- How colour is used to show the passage of time.
- The use of juxtapositions (e.g. the knife and the chicken, violence and celebration).
- How Lil Ze's power in the favela is represented.
- The linking of the gun and the camera.

It's been that way ever since I was a kid.

Revising representations of gender, age and ethnicity in *City of God*

Activity
Representations of gender

Read the following extract from Jennie Carlsten's article, 'Violence in the *City of God*: The Fantasy of the Omniscient Spectator' (2006).

> 'The favela is also a site of gendered violence. The City of God *is represented as almost exclusively male, and women's bodies simply provide another site for the men to carry out violence against one another. Meirelles includes women primarily as victims, such as Shorty's wife. After her husband catches her with another man (who flees), he beats her with a shovel, and then buries her alive. The rape of Ned's girlfriend (also unnamed) is framed less as a complete act in itself, but as the instigation of violence, sparking off the full-scale gang war at the film's conclusion. The strongest women of the film, Angelica and Bernice, attempt to reverse this power equation by using their sexual hold over the men, encouraging them to leave the gangs; they are unsuccessful. Both lose the man as a result of his escape attempts, making them both indirect victims of the violence, and indirectly responsible for it.'*

Write a response to this, stating whether you agree or disagree with Carlsten's argument. Make references to the film and key female characters Angelica and Bernice in your response.

Activity
Representations of masculinity

The three main male characters, Rocket, Lil Ze and Benny, all have divergent paths despite being raised in the same social conditions. Each character offers a different portrayal of masculinity, from violent and toxic (Lil Ze) to enterprising and moral (Rocket). For each character, give examples of how they represent different facets of masculinity. Consider what happens to each character over the course of the narrative.

Character	Representations of masculinity
Rocket	

Lil Ze

Benny

Revision activity

On YouTube watch the video 'Director Fernando Meirelles Discusses the Making of *City of God*.'

Answer the following questions:

1. How did *City of God* secure finance?

2. How does the financing of the film contrast to how mainstream Hollywood films are financed?

3. What were the reasons behind some of the decisions made on how to tell the story?

Activity
Representations of children

Write a report on how children are represented in *City of God*. Use the following questions to structure your report:

- What is the quality of life like for children growing up in the favelas? What key issues affect children in these spaces?
- How are the runts represented in *City of God*? Does the film suggest they are victims of circumstance?
- How does the representation of children in *City of God* compare with Western ideals of childhood and children as innocent and naive?
- How does the film remind us that the runts are just children, despite having to deal with adult issues and extreme violence?

Revising the contexts of *City of God*

Activity
Cultural and institutional contexts

City of God was successful in Brazil and in the West. Director Meirelles commented that: '*It was a huge success in Brazil and attracted 3.4 million spectators. It was more popular than "Star Wars" and "Minority Report". It moved from the cultural pages to the political pages – one of the presidential candidates asked to see the film and talked about it in a speech. So teenage drug-dealing became an issue in the campaign.*'

Create a knowledge organiser on the film's success and its place within Brazilian cinema and South American cinema more generally. Include:

- Local and global box office figures for *City of God*.
- Reasons why the film was so successful locally and globally. Discuss how although *City of God* is culturally Brazilian and draws on *Cinema Novo*, there are crossovers with Hollywood film.
- Why the Weinstein company distributed the film – how it fits in with their brand identity.
- Points on globalisation and the popularity of South American cinema – give examples of other successful films released in the same period as *City of God* such as *Amores Perros* (Iñárritu, 2000)

Social, political contexts and ethnicity

Search online for the *Guardian* article 'Why I Love ... the Depiction of the Favela in *City of God*' by Jo Griffin.

The favelas of Rio de Janerio

Use the article and your own analysis of *City of God* to create a PowerPoint presentation on the representations of the favelas and its peoples. Include:

- Information about the favelas of Brazil.
- Explanation of the social conditions in the favelas.
- Information on the drug gangs in the favelas.
- How the favelas and drug wars are represented in *City of God*.
- How the favelas are represented as having mainly poor black residents, with some ethnic diversity.
- How *City of God* represents life outside the favelas – e.g. when Rocket stays with the middle-class, white reporter.
- A comparison of tourist websites and adverts of Rio de Janeiro and the alternative representation of the area in *City of God*.

Visual style and social contexts

Go to the following website: www.cinemahumain.com/city-of-god/

Read the article 'How does the visual style of *City of God* draw attention to social realities in Brazil?' by Reina-Marie Loader

- Write a brief summary of the main points of the article.
- Give three new insights you have gained about how the visual style of *City of God* conveys social themes and issues.

Key sequence analysis: 'The Story of the Apartment'

Write or record an audio commentary analysing the core areas of film form, representations and contexts in 'The Story of the Apartment' sequence.

Use the bullet points below to help structure your commentary:

- The purpose of the fixed-camera position.
- Use of dissolves.
- Use of the wide-angled lens.
- The move from a feminine to a hyper-masculine and violent space.
- How mise-en-scène and lighting reflect the changes in the apartment from a homely to a dangerous place.
- How the sequence provides exposition in a stylised and engaging way.
- How this sequence conveys the overall messages of the film about how drugs and gangs had a destructive impact on the favelas in Rio de Janeiro.

Sample essay on aesthetics in *Mustang* and *Taxi Tehran*

Brief but relevant introduction

My two chosen films are *Mustang* and *Taxi Tehran*. In both films, aesthetic qualities convey key themes and messages and are interlinked with the specific contexts in which the films were produced. Both films therefore have a powerful political and social impact.

Focused on the question of aesthetic impact

Mustang's aesthetic of freedom and entrapment, conveying the message that young girls in rural Turkey are oppressed by religious patriarchal conservativism, is evident throughout the film. The opening sequences display the aesthetics of freedom in rural Turkey before the girls are married off, when an aesthetic of imprisonment takes over. In the opening sequences, the girls are in long-shot in the sea, often framed together as one. This was an aesthetic choice by director Ergüven, who wanted the girls to be viewed as one unit before they are married off, when they start to be framed separately. The outdoor long-shots of the girls playing in the wide expansive sea convey childhood freedom. These juxtapose with later shots of the girls imprisoned in the home, with the mise-en-scène of bars on windows and high walls creating an oppressive environment. This imprisonment aesthetic therefore makes Lale and Nur's escape even more impactful as they finally find freedom through journeying to Istanbul.

Detailed filmic references

The creative choice to use handheld cameras, location shooting in rural Anatolia and non-professional actors throughout creates a realist aesthetic essential for the film's political message, that a patriarchal religious conservatism limits women's freedom, is the reality for girls in rural areas of Turkey. The moments where the girls find moments of freedom are made all the more impactful through the use of visuals and sound. For instance, when the girls attend the football match, the loud sound of girls on the bus laughing and stamping their feet are in contrast to the quiet area where they live. Slow-motion is used to capture and preserve these brief moments of happiness. This nostalgic aesthetic is also heightened by the use of bright lighting around the girls.

Links to the film's messages and themes

The handheld 'shoot and run' aesthetic is also made more impactful when considering the production contexts in which the film was made. There is a sense of urgency in the scene where Ece has sex in the car due to the fact that the film was shot in a very conservative area, therefore the filmmakers had to adopt guerrilla filming methods for scenes such as this so as not to draw attention to filming and upset local people. The quick handheld shots thus emphasise the forbidden nature of Ece having sex and the rebellious nature of the act and fear of getting caught.

Contextual knowledge applied appropriately

The aesthetics of *Taxi Tehran* were also shaped by the film's political and production contexts. As director Jafar Panahi was banned from making films, he decided to shoot from inside his car and create a film about the lives of people in Tehran through his interactions with various passengers in the taxi. The aesthetic limitations make the aesthetic all the more impactful as it demonstrates how certain Iranian filmmakers find creative ways to produce their films due to the restrictions on them. Panahi works around these limitations by using dash-cams inside his car, therefore creating more close-ups and mid-shots of the passengers, which creates an intimacy and offers images of both the passengers and Tehran from the perspective of the car window. This realism offers us a real-life view of Tehran, as people outside, apart from the boy in Hannah's story, were unaware that a film was being made. The aesthetic of the melding of public and the private is conveyed through the use of the cameras inside the car as passengers get in and out.

Focused on the question of aesthetic impact

The realist aesthetic is heightened through the self-reflexive nature of the film as certain characters, including Panahi himself, play versions of themselves. The human rights lawyer plays herself and is aware she is being filmed, as she looks into the camera, breaking the fourth wall, giving the film a documentary vérité aesthetic. She leaves a rose in the car for the people of Iran, offering a beauty and optimising to the aesthetic, emphasised in the final shot when Panahi leaves the car and we view him from the windscreen, walking off into the distance with the rose in the foreground, offering a sense of hope for increased freedoms and equality for the people of Iran.

Focused on the question of aesthetic impact

The use of longer takes and little non-diegetic sound throughout the films is made all the more impactful when understood in the context of Iranian New Wave cinema, with offers a more contemplative cinema. Indeed, the aesthetic and conceit of *Taxi Tehran* is inspired by the father of Iranian cinema, Kiarostami, particularly his film *Ten*, about a woman driver and her conversations with passengers. The notion that Iranian cinema is 'poor on the outside but rich on the inside' is wholly appropriate to *Taxi Tehran*, as through a simple conceit and camera set-up, the film offers us a rich understanding of the cross-section of people in Tehran, their concerns and competing views. The sequences with Hanna offer us a perspective on the restrictions facing filmmakers, as Hanna, who wants to be a filmmaker, explains what she cannot film in order to make a film distributable.

Application of contextual knowledge and understanding

Overall, the aesthetic qualities of both films enhance their realism and remind the audience that the films represented the lives of ordinary peoples in those nations and the issues they face.

Brief but relevant conclusion

Finish it

Complete the following practice 40-mark exam question response on global film using *Pan's Labyrinth* and *City of God*. The first short paragraph is written for you. Refer to two key sequences from each film.

How are mise-en-scène and/or performance used in meaningful ways in the films you have studied?

In *Pan's Labyrinth*, mise-en-scène is used in symbolic ways to convey the film's themes, including childhood trauma during times of war, the violence and evil of fascism. It also uses gothic fairy tale imagery partly influenced by the paintings of Goya and Freudian imagery in symbolic ways to represent fertility and womanhood. In *City of God*, non-actors and improvisation are used to enhance the performances to give the film a realism despite the heavily stylised nature of the film.

Documentary film

What to revise

The core areas:

Film form: cinematography, mise-en,scene, sound, editing and performance

Representations and **aesthetics**

Social, cultural, political, historical and institutional (including production) contexts

The key areas you will be assessed on are:

- The **core areas**: film form (cinematography, mise-en-scène, editing, sound and performance); representations (ethnicity, gender and age) and aesthetics; and contexts.
- **Specialist area: Critical debates**: the significance of **digital technology** in film.
- **Specialist area: Filmmakers' theories**: you will be expected to apply ONE of the following filmmakers' theories to the documentary film you have studied: Peter Watkins, Nick Broomfield, Kim Longinotto or Michael Moore.

How you will be assessed at A Level

- You choose one essay question from a choice of two.
- The question is worth **20 marks**.

How to approach a 20-mark question on documentary film

- We recommend that you spend 30 minutes maximum answering the question (including planning time).
- This is a fairly short essay. Keep to the point and only include analysis that is relevant to the question.
- You only need to provide a very short introduction and conclusion.
- Focus on one or two sequences in detail.
- If you are answering a question on filmmakers' theories, use **one** filmmaker's theory and apply it to a key sequence from the film you have studied.
- Look at the examples of annotated responses to questions on documentary on page 121.

Revising the core areas of documentary

Activity

Documentary techniques

In the following table are some of the most common techniques used in documentary filmmaking. For each technique, provide a definition and give an example of how the technique is used (if relevant) in the documentary film you have studied. You can check the answers on page 231 of the textbook.

Technique	Definition	Example
Direct and indirect interviews		
Archival footage		
Talking heads		
Voice-over or narration		

Now complete the table below using three other techniques that are used in the documentary film you have studied:

Technique	Definition	Example

Knowledge booster quiz

A common technique used by documentary filmmakers is **frankenbiting**. Search for this term online, then answer the following questions:

1. Define frankenbiting.

2. Explain why documentary filmmakers use frankenbiting.

3. Give an example of where frankenbiting is used in the documentary film you have studied.

Activity

How documentary combines non-fiction and fiction techniques

Recent documentaries often combine techniques associated with non-fiction and fiction films. Documentary filmmakers are increasingly making us aware that documentaries are just as constructed as fiction films.

In his book *Introduction to Documentary* (2010), film academic Bill Nichols created this Venn diagram to show the areas of convergence between fiction and non-fiction:

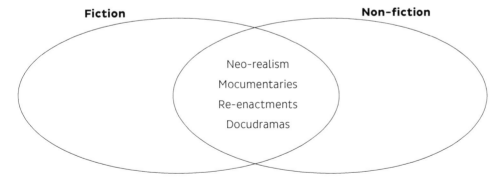

Complete the Venn diagram, listing genres and techniques used in fiction filmmaking and techniques used in non-fiction filmmaking.

Apply the Venn diagram to the documentary film you have studied. Answer the following questions:

- What genres and techniques associated with fiction filmmaking are used in the documentary film you have studied? Give examples from the film.
- What genres and techniques associated with non-fiction filmmaking are used in the documentary film you have studied? Give examples from the film.
- Give examples of where fiction and non-fiction genres and techniques are combined.

Revision activity

Institutional contexts of documentary film.

The **Sheffield Doc Fest** is an annual festival premiering international documentary films. Look at the website for the festival, then answer the following questions:

1. Why are film festivals important for documentary filmmakers?

2. How does the festival showcase and promote films directed by women and people from different ethnic backgrounds?

Activity

Documentary modes

Provide a brief definition for each documentary mode.

Mode	Definition
Poetic	
Expository	
Observational	
Participatory	
Reflexive	
Performative	

Activity

Documentary modes of the film you have studied

Create a poster for the modes used in the documentary film you have studied. Include:

- A description of the modes used with still images from the film.
- Annotated stills from the film with bullet points on how and why certain modes are used.
- Examples of where different modes are combined.

Activity

The institutional contexts of documentary

Documentary film had a revival in the 1990s. Film studies scholar Linda Williams stated that documentaries have '*unprecedented popularity among general audiences, who now line up for documentaries as eagerly as they do fiction films*' ('Mirrors without Memories', *Film Quarterly*, 1993).

List some of the reasons why documentaries are still popular with audiences. Consider:

- Subject matter
- Key popular documentary filmmakers.

Some well-known documentary films, such as Michael Moore's *Fahrenheit 9/11* (2004), were successful at the box office. Think about where you now typically see and experience documentary films. Answer the following question:

- Which are some of the major companies that invest in and distribute documentary films?

Find out the budget for the documentary film you have studied, then answer the following questions:

- What was the budget for the film?
- How does the budget compare to a mainstream Hollywood fiction film?

Revising the specialist area: critical debates: the significance of digital technology in film

The specification says:

The degree of the impact that digital has had on film since the 1990s is a developing debate. Some film commentators argue that, although digital technology could potentially transform cinema, so far films, especially narrative films designed for cinema release, have changed very little from pre-digital times. Others consider that the impact of digital filmmaking is only beginning to emerge, both in high concept Hollywood filmmaking and in much lower budget experimental work.

Activity

On YouTube, watch the short video essay 'Film vs Digital' by Toby Kearton. Although the video essay focuses on fiction film, the debates about the shift from celluloid to digital filmmaking are still relevant to documentary filmmaking. After watching the video essay, make a list of the advantages and disadvantages of digital filmmaking identified in the video.

Activity

Choose a sequence from the documentary film you have studied that uses digital technology in interesting ways. Identify the digital technologies used, then state the impact of the digital technology on the spectator.

Description of the key sequence	Digital technologies used	Impact of digital technology on the spectator

Practice essay question on digital debates in documentary

How is digital technology used to create an emotional impact on the spectator in the documentary film you have studied?

- When answering the question, think about how digital technology may be used to manipulate images and sound to create certain effects.
- Set a timer for 30 minutes for each question to practise exam timings.
- Refer to a key sequence from the documentary film you have studied.
- Look at the mark scheme in the WJEC Eduqas Specimen Assessment Materials (online) and assess your own work.
- Consider swapping essays with a fellow student and marking each other's response.

Revising the specialist area: filmmakers' theories

The specification says:

The documentary film will be explored in relation to key filmmakers from the genre. The documentary film studied may either directly embody aspects of these theories or work in a way that strongly challenges these theories. In either case, the theories will provide a means of exploring different approaches to documentary film and filmmaking.

The filmmakers selected for study are not academics. We therefore recommend that you interpret 'filmmakers' theories', as the documentary filmmakers' **approaches** and **ideas**.

Revision activity

Watch the documentary film *Side by Side* (Kenneally, 2012), which examines the impact of digital technology on filmmaking.

Make bullet-point notes on how digital technology has affected and changed the filmmaking process.

Revision activity

Choose one sequence from the documentary film you have studied. Storyboard the sequence in the style and approach of one of the four filmmakers' theories you have studied. This activity will help you to compare the filmmaker's approach/theory to the documentary film you have studied.

Choose one or two filmmakers whose theories/approaches you have studied.

In the table below, provide a bullet-point summary of their theories/approaches to documentary filmmaking and some examples of their notable films:

Filmmaker	Theories/approaches and key films
Peter Watkins	
Nick Broomfield	
Kim Longinotto	
Michael Moore	

Activity

Use the table you have completed above, your class notes and interviews with your documentary filmmaker (you can search for these online), to create a poster on one filmmaker whose theory/approach you have studied. Include the following on your poster:

- Annotated stills from key films which demonstrate the filmmaker's approach/theory.
- Key quotations from the filmmaker interviews about their approach to documentary film.

Practice essay question on filmmakers' theories

How far does the documentary film you have studied reflect the ideas of one filmmaker's theory?

- Refer in detail to a sequence from the documentary film you have studied.
- You do not need to compare the films or the filmmaker's theory with the film you have studied. Only apply their approach and mention their films briefly. Stay focused on the film you have studied.
- Set a timer for 30 minutes for each question to practise exam timings.
- Look at the mark scheme in the WJEC Eduqas Specimen Assessment Materials (online) and assess your own work.
- Consider swapping essays with a fellow student and marking each other's response.
- You can read a sample annotated response for this question on page 121. The response uses *Amy* and Kim Longinotto as a Case study.

Stories We Tell (Polley, 2013)

Revising the core areas of *Stories We Tell*

Techniques used in *Stories We Tell*

Sarah Polley uses a variety of documentary techniques to make us aware of the constructed nature of filmmaking. For each technique used, state how it is commonly used in documentaries and then how Polley uses it in *Stories We Tell*. Give specific examples from the film.

The first example is completed for you:

Technique	How it is commonly used in documentary	How Polley uses this technique
Handheld camera	*Creates authenticity. Often used when filming real events as they happen.*	*Reconstructions on Super 8 are handheld to make them look authentic and fool the spectator into thinking the footage is real. Gives the impression of real home footage shot by an amateur filmmaker, e.g. the shaky camera and blurred images of play rehearsals give a voyeuristic and amateur-shot feel to the scene.*
Voice-over narration		
Talking heads		
Archive footage and photographs		
Reconstructions or re-enactments		

Representations of gender

Watch sequences from Sarah Polley's fiction films *Away From Her* (2006) and *Take this Waltz* (2011). Note any comparisons in themes and aesthetics to *Stories We Tell*.

Re-watch the sequence where each family member discusses how George gaining custody of the children affected Diane (approx. 49 minutes into the film). Answer the following questions:

- How did the media at the time represent and judge Diane? Look at the images from the newspaper clippings.
- How do Diane's children's accounts of their mother compare with the representations of Diane in the newspapers published at the time?
- What techniques are used to evoke sympathy with Diane's situation and its impact on her children?

Search online for Leah Anderst's article 'Memory's Chorus: *Stories We Tell* and Sarah Polley's Theory of Autobiography' (2013) in *Senses of Cinema* (online).

List the key arguments on how Polley uses many stories to get closer to the truth.

Activity

Cultural contexts

Stories We Tell reflects a wider trend of documentaries that question the nature of objective reality and memory. Examples include *The Thin Blue Line* (Morris, 1988), *Capturing the Friedmans* (Jarecki, 2003) and *The Imposter* (Layton, 2012). These films all have a fascination with the fragmented nature of memory. They do not try to offer an objective reality, instead they recognise that the truth is subjective, that there is no one single 'truth'. Critics identify Errol Morris as starting this trend with *The Thin Blue Line*.

Linda Williams identifies the following characteristics of this new mode of documentary filmmaking in *The Thin Blue Line* ('Mirrors without Memories', *Film Quarterly*, 1993):

- The use of re-enactments by actors
- Individuals or characters have competing and differing narratives
- A deliberate abandonment of voyeuristic objectivity
- Interviews are in a confessional mode, like a therapy session
- People's memories of past events are like fragments – memory is not always clear or reliable; people may have different memories of the same event
- The narrative moves forward and back in time – it is non-linear.

List the characteristics of New Documentary as identified by Williams that are relevant to *Stories We Tell*. Give examples from the film for each characteristic.

Institutional contexts

Stories We Tell was funded by the National Film Board of Canada and the Canadian Film Centre.

The National Film Board of Canada (NFB) describe themselves as *'the nation's public producer and distributor of distinctive and audacious audiovisual content. Our mandate is to engage Canadians and the world through the production of creative and innovative works that reflect our country and Canadian points of view.'*

Look at the website for the National Film Board of Canada at www.nfb.ca and answer the following questions:

- What kinds of documentary films do the NFB fund and support?
- Why do you think the NFB supported and co-funded *Stories We Tell?*

The Canadian Film Centre (CFC) *'supports, develops and accelerates the content, careers and companies of Canadian creative and entrepreneurial talent in the screen-based and digital industries'* (CFC online). Look at the 'About' section on the CFC website www.cfccreates.com and answer the following questions:

- How is the CFC funded?
- What are the CFC's main aims and goals?

Have a look at the 'Programs/film' section of the website and answer the following questions:

- What kind of films do the CFC fund?
- How do the CFC support emerging talent?
- Why do you think the CFC supported and co-funded *Stories We Tell?*

Digital debates

Stories We Tell combines the use of digital cameras, Super 8 and 16mm footage. Use the still images and your own experience of watching the film to answer the following question:

- What different aesthetic effects are created by the use of Super 8 and digital cameras?

Knowledge booster quiz

In the 'home movie' footage in *Stories We Tell*, Polley uses the Super 8 film format.

Research Super 8, then answer the following questions:

1. What is Super 8?
2. In which decades was Super 8 the most popular format for shooting home movies?
3. Why did Polley choose to use this format?

Revision activity

Search on YouTube for *'Stories We Tell* Director Sarah Polley in Studio Q'. Watch the interview and answer the following questions:

1. What was the main reason for making the film?
2. What was Polley's inspiration for the film?
3. Why was Polley keen to show as many contradictory accounts of her mother Diane?

Filmmakers' theories: Michael Moore

We will apply **Michael Moore**'s approach to documentary filmmaking to *Stories We Tell*.

Activity

Read the following description of Michael Moore's theory/approach from the specification:

> Michael Moore is a very visible presence in his documentaries, which can thus be described as **participatory** and **performative**. His work is highly committed – overtly **polemical** in taking up a clear point of view, what might be called **agit-prop documentary**. He justifies his practice in terms of providing 'balance' for mainstream media that, in his view, provides false information. Part of Moore's approach is to use humour, sometimes to lampoon the subject of his work and sometimes to recognise that documentaries need to entertain and hold an audience.

- Give a brief definition of all the words in bold. Research online for definitions and explanations.

Activity

Watch two or three sequences from some of Michael Moore's most notable films. These include:

- *Roger & Me* (1989)
- *Bowling for Columbine* (2002)
- *Fahrenheit 9/11* (2004)
- *Capitalism: A Love Story* (2009)
- *Where to Invade Next* (2015)
- *Fahrenheit 11/9* (2018).

Now choose one sequence from any one of Moore's films that best exemplifies his approach to filmmaking. Then complete the following activities:

- Create a poster using stills from the sequence to demonstrate his approach to filmmaking.
- Complete the Venn diagram to show how Michael Moore is similar to and departs from Sarah Polley's approach to *Stories We Tell*.

Revision activity

Search on YouTube for 'Sheffield Doc/Fest 2016: The Channel 4 Interview with **Michael Moore**'.

Watch the interview and make notes on Michael Moore's motivation and approach to making documentary films.

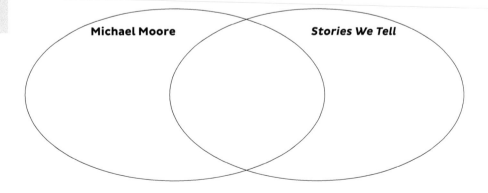

Key sequence analysis: Sarah meets Harry

Re-watch the sequence where Sarah meets Harry and discovers he is her biological father. Write a 300-word analysis of the sequence, applying the core and specialist areas. Use the bullet points and still images below to help you focus on key areas.

Core areas

- Use of sound – silent film piano music
- The impact of Michael's voice-over
- Lack of sound over the re-construction of Harry and Sarah's meeting
- The use of grainy image and handheld camera for reconstructions
- Performance – how Harry and Sally perform their first meeting
- Aesthetics – how film techniques create a nostalgic, home-movie and personal aesthetic
- Representations – the establishing of a 'father–daughter' relationship between Harry and Sarah
- Contexts – how the film offers a more liberal and complex analysis of what constitutes a family.

Digital debates

- The contrast between sharper digital images used in interviews and the use of Super 8 reconstructions.

Filmmaker's theory

- Comparisons between the film and the filmmaker's approach you have studied. Think about what the filmmaker may do differently from Polley.

> ### Activity
>
> Read the sample annotated response on *Stories We Tell* in the textbook on page 249 (Aaron's response). Complete the response with reference to another scene from *Stories We Tell*. Provide a short conclusion of one or two sentences.

Amy (Kapadia, 2005)

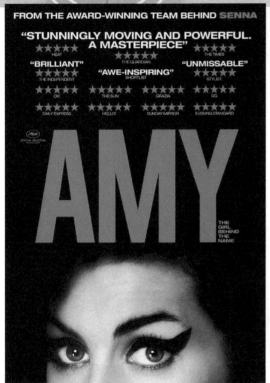

FROM THE AWARD-WINNING TEAM BEHIND SENNA

"STUNNINGLY MOVING AND POWERFUL.
A MASTERPIECE"
★★★★★
HEAT
★★★★★
THE TIMES

"BRILLIANT"
★★★★★
THE INDEPENDENT
"AWE-INSPIRING"
★★★★★
SHORTLIST
"UNMISSABLE"
★★★★★
STYLIST

★★★★★
OK!
★★★★★
THE SUN
★★★★★
GRAZIA
★★★★★
GQ

★★★★★
DAILY EXPRESS
★★★★★
HELLO!
★★★★★
SUNDAY MIRROR
★★★★★
EVENING STANDARD

AMY

THE
GIRL
BEHIND
THE
NAME

Knowledge booster

Institutional contexts of *Amy*

These facts will help increase your
knowledge of the institutional
contexts of the film:

- *Amy* took 24 million dollars at
  the worldwide box office.
- When making documentaries,
  Kapadia doesn't have a
  treatment, logline, or script –
  he lets the story form from the
  footage.
- Kapadia usually shows people
  versions of the film, including
  the very long versions before
  cutting it down to the final,
  shorter form.

Revising the core areas of *Amy*

The use of music and imagery

Director Asif Kapadia read Amy Winehouse's lyrics and understood
that they are personal and tell her story:

> 'My family background is in India and Bollywood films use songs to
> tell narrative. Clearly Amy is not here to talk to, but we do have her
> songs and her lyrics which are very personal and in the film, they
> become her voice to help us understand what was going on in her
> head.'

Kapadia linked Amy's voice with footage of the people in her life
whom the lyrics are about. In this sense, it can be argued that Amy
Winehouse is a 'narrator'.

Re-watch the scene 'Love is a Losing Game' (78 minutes in).

Write a 200-word analysis of the use of sound and imagery in this
sequence. Comment on:

- The impact of seeing the handwritten lyrics on screen
- What the lyrics reveal about Amy's state of mind and her
  relationship with Blake
- The use of slow-motion footage of Amy and Blake
- The use of close-ups of Amy during her performance.

Amy and 'true fiction'

Kapadia has described his style of documentary filmmaking as 'True
Fiction'. He states that he makes films, not documentaries.

- Define 'True Fiction'? Is this an oxymoron?
- List some of the ways in which *Amy* differs from conventional
  documentaries.

Social and cultural contexts

Kapadia's trilogy of documentary films, *Senna*, *Amy* and *Maradona*, are about talented and tragic young people who grew up in the media spotlight. The 'characters' in these three films are outsiders who are fighting a powerful system. Kapadia has stated that the documentaries are about the characters' journey as the audience already knows the ending.

Revision activity

Kapadia started making the film a year after Amy died. He described it as a raw film and an emotional experience:

'You become part of the story and character.' Amy's friends often cried while being interviewed.

How does this sense of rawness, shock and grief manifest in the film? Give examples from some of the interviews conducted with Amy's friends and family.

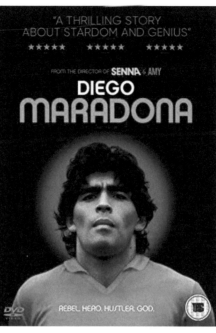

Search online for trailers and clips from *Senna* (Kapadia, 2010) and *Diego Maradona* (Kapadia, 2019).

Create a poster using annotated stills to compare all three films. Include:

- How the films capture the lives of famous people in the late 20th and early 21st century in a media-saturated environment
- Representations of age, gender and ethnicity
- The similarities in style – e.g. use of archival footage to tell a personal story
- How all three characters are positioned as outsiders.

Activity

Representations of gender, ethnicity and age

Complete the table below to explore the ways in which Amy is represented in the film. Give specific examples from key sequences or moments in the film.

Representations	Representations and examples from the film
Age: representations of Amy as a young, tragic star	
Ethnicity: representations of Amy's Jewish identity	
Gender: representations of how Amy is treated as a young woman	

Representations of Mitch Winehouse

Search online for the WJEC EDUQAS Documentary resources on *Amy*.

Download the PDF titled '*Amy* Case study – Student Copy'. Complete the activities contained in the booklet.

Amy's father, Mitch Winehouse, argued that: '*The film is representing me in a not very good way. There is no balance … It's portraying me and Amy in not a very good light.*'

Kapadia responded to these criticisms with: '*The clue is in the title. It is a film about her, and I think at various points of her life, a lot of people made decisions which were not about her and not in her best interests. And even now there are people who kind of think it's about them, and it's not about them.*'

Give arguments in bullet-point form for and against the notion that Mitch Winehouse is represented unfairly in *Amy*. Give examples from the film as evidence for your arguments.

Digital debates

Approximately 90% of the footage used in *Amy* is digital. Much of the personal footage of Amy was taken on home video and digital smartphones by her friends. Kapadia had this to say about the use of smartphones:

'This is more personal because this is becoming home movies, and by the end of it, it's camera phones. But people have always been recording what's going on around them in one form or another. It's just a question of whether you know where to look and whether or not people have kept that format.

Strangely enough, the older formats of film last longer than digital, because (now) we delete photos, we delete video, we delete our audio interviews. People used to keep everything because they had a cassette tape. Now when you interview somebody, how often do you keep that audio once you've used it?'

Use this quote and your own knowledge of digital footage used in *Amy* to write a 300-word commentary on the use of digital footage.

Comment on:

- How video and personal smartphone footage is used to create a personal connection to Amy
- Examples of where Kapadia uses footage from Amy's gigs shot by audience members on smartphones
- The use of paparazzi shots and personal images of Amy and Blake addicted to drugs
- The digital manipulation of sound in sequences such as the 'Back to Black' sequence.

Watch Mark Kermode's review of *Amy* on YouTube.

Answer the following questions:

1. **What does Kermode argue are the strengths of the film?**

2. **What does Kermode argue is the impact of recording audio interviews?**

3. **Why does Kermode find the paparazzi footage so heart-breaking to watch?**

Filmmakers' theories: Kim Longinotto

We will apply **Kim Longinotto**'s approach to documentary filmmaking to *Amy*.

Activity

Read the following description of Kim Longinotto's approach/theory in the specification:

> 'Longinotto has said "I don't think of films as documents or records of things. I try to make them as like the experience of watching a fiction film as possible, though, of course, nothing is ever set up." Her work is about finding characters that the audience will identify with – "you can make this jump into someone else's experience". Longinotto is invisible, with very little use of voice-over, formal interviews, captions or incidental music. As the "eyes" of her audience, she doesn't like to zoom or pan. She says she doesn't want her films to have conclusions but to raise questions.'

Watch two or three sequences from the following films directed by Longinotto:

- *Divorce Iranian Style* (1998)
- *Sisters in Law* (2005)
- *Dreamcatcher* (2015).

Use the description from the specification, sequences from other Longinotto films, and your own research to complete the following activities:

- Create a poster using stills from the sequences to demonstrate Longinotto's approach to filmmaking.
- Complete the Venn diagram below to show how Kim Longinotto is similar to and departs from Kapadia's approach to *Amy*.

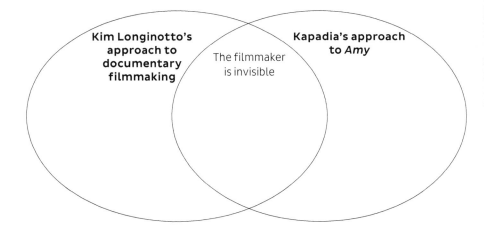

Kim Longinotto's approach to documentary filmmaking

The filmmaker is invisible

Kapadia's approach to *Amy*

Knowledge booster quiz

On the BFI YouTube channel, watch 'Ask a documentary filmmaker: Kim Longinotto'. Answer the following questions:

1. Why does Longinotto think it's important to work closely with an editor?

2. What is Longinotto's approach to filming the human subjects of her documentary?

3. What films and directors have influenced Longinotto?

Key sequence analysis: the Grammy Awards

Re-watch the sequence where Amy wins a Grammy Award, then write or record an audio commentary applying the core and specialist areas. Use the bullet points and still images to help you focus on key areas. Consider:

Core areas

- Use of archival footage and documents
- Use of slow-motion
- How the non-diegetic score enhances the feeling of sadness
- How Juliette Ashby's voice-over offers a new perspective on the celebrations
- Representations of Amy as a tragic figure not fully in control of her own life
- How elements of film form are combined to create a personal and 'true fiction' aesthetic.

Filmmakers' theories

- Comparisons between the film and the filmmaker's approach you have studied. Think about how the filmmaker you have studied may use different techniques.

Digital debates

- The use of digital cameras to shoot Amy's performance
- How digital technology creates sharp, focused images.

Sample essay on filmmaker's theory and *Amy*

The following essay is composed using extracts from an exemplar response for a 20-mark question on documentary film. It is authored by A Level Film Studies teacher and expert John Fitzgerald.

Demonstrates knowledge and understanding of filmmaker's approach

Throughout the documentary, '*Amy*', there are uses of observational cinema named by the filmmaker, Kim Longinotto. Her work often highlights the plight of female victims of oppression and depression, finding characters that the audience will identify with, the stories which she documents are all uniquely personal, mainly focusing on society's outsiders. This theory of observational filmmaking, also known as direct cinema, usually excludes certain documentary techniques such as advanced planning, scripting, narration and interviewing.

This is relevant to the documentary, 'Amy', as Asif Kapadia uses observational filmmaking in 'Amy' to aim to encourage spectators to feel the loss, and grieve Amy. A good example of this observation cinema is in the last scene of the documentary, Amy's death and aftermath. The scene outside of Amy's funeral is extremely similar to Longinotto's way of filming, as the director, in this moment, just lets the footage tell the story without including any extra features, like a voice-over or interviews. This creates a melancholy atmosphere and lets the death sink in for the spectators, allows them time to look back on this icon's life and realise what a great loss it was. However, Kapadia does use features that are not included in observational cinema, such as interviews and voice-overs.

Application of knowledge to *Amy* with focus on a key sequence

In the sequence 'Back to Black', Kapadia uses voice-overs and on-screen text. The voice-over of Mark Ronson, allows us to see Amy from his perspective showing the audience the reality of her life and that no matter how far she fell into her addiction, her love for music never decreased and she continued to try and enjoy doing what she loved. This scene is extremely successful in isolating Amy, mainly through Kapadia's use of strong, bold lines, provided by the booth in which she is in to record the song, almost trapping her inside a small box. By doing this, Kapadia emphasises her loneliness, which allows the spectator to view her as a human being, not only a star and provides them with the details of how much her songs actually reflect her life and tell her personal experiences. Moreover, this is supported by the speech used at the end of the scene when at the end of the song Amy responds 'that's a bit upsetting at the end isn't it' as if she's trying to demote her emotion and escape her depression by making it sound accidental. On the narrative as a whole, this sequence shows Amy at her peak and its narrative function is developmental, it also gives us the knowledge of her impending death.

Detailed analysis of a key sequence

Understanding of the emotional impact of the scene and techniques used

Finish it

Complete the following practice 20-mark exam question response on documentary film, using *Amy*. The first two short paragraphs are written for you. Aim to use two key sequences from each film.

How important is digital technology in the construction of the documentary film you have studied?

In *Amy*, Kapadia relies on archive footage to construct the tragic story of the life and career of Amy Winehouse. Over 90% of the archival footage is digital, using personal footage shot on Amy's friends' smartphones and audience members who attended her gigs and shot the footage on their phones.

The sequences after the opening credits demonstrate this use of digital, smartphone footage.

Film movements: Silent cinema

What you need to revise

The core areas:

- **Film form**: cinematography, mise-en-scène, sound, editing and performance
- **Representations** and **aesthetics**
- Social, cultural, political, historical and institutional (including production) **contexts**.

The specialist area:

- Critical debates: **the realist and the expressive**.

How you will be assessed at A Level

In the examination, you will choose one question out of a choice of two. The question is worth **20 marks**.

You are assessed on your knowledge and understanding of the silent film or films you have studied. You should be able to discuss the film as an example of a **film movement of the 1920s**. You could be asked a question about the specialist area where you should discuss the film or films as an example of a realist and/or an expressive mode of filmmaking.

How to approach a 20-mark question on silent cinema

- We recommend that you spend 30 minutes maximum answering the question (including planning time).
- This is a fairly short essay. Keep focused on the question.
- Keep your introduction and conclusion short and to the point.
- Focus on one or two sequences from your chosen silent film or films. If you have studied the four Buster Keaton short films, we recommend you choose one or two relevant sequences from any of the four films.
- Contextualise the film within its appropriate film movement.

We will revise the specialist area, then focus on *Sunrise* (Murnau, 1927) and the four Buster Keaton short films as case studies.

Revising film movements

You will have studied one of the following silent film movements:

- **American silent film comedy:** Buster Keaton short films (1920-1922)
- **German Expressionism:** *Sunrise* **or** *Spione/Spies* (Lang, 1928)
- **Constructivism and montage:** *Strike* (Eisenstein, 1924) **or** *Man with a Movie Camera* (Vertov, 1928) **AND** *À Propos de Nice* (Vigo, 1930).

Patrick Phillips defines film movements as:

'a **distinctive body of films**, each directed by an **auteur**. It is often further constituted by a related **body of critical or theoretical writing**. A film movement will be of significance in film history because **of thematic and formal/stylistic innovations** which characterise the films and which are, most often, **a response to wider political, social or cultural changes** at a particular time and in a particular place.'

Film movements

Use Patrick Phillips' definition on the previous page to help you answer the questions below about the film movement you have studied:

- What are the defining characteristics of your film movement?
- Who are the key filmmakers of the movement and why are they significant?
- What are some of the most influential and well-known films of the movement?
- To what extent are the silent film or films you have studied typical of the film movement?
- How is a film movement different from a film genre or national cinema? Are there any overlaps between these terms?

Revising the specialist area of the realist and the expressive

The specification says:

> 'In the 1940s, the French film critic André Bazin set in motion a major debate when he argued that both German Expressionist and Soviet Montage filmmaking went against what he saw as the "realist" calling of cinema. This opposition between the realist and the expressive has informed thinking about film from the beginnings of cinema when the documentary realism of the Lumière Brothers was set in opposition to the fantasy films of Méliès.'

Bazin believed that cinema should aim to show an objective reality through filmic devices such as long takes and deep focus. Bazin was opposed to montage-style editing and exaggerated mise-en-scène as seen in German Expressionist films as he believed this did not represent the world as it is.

The realist and the expressive

Answer the following questions with references to the silent film or films you have studied:

- Define a realist cinema. Give examples of realism in the silent film or films you have studied.
- Define an expressive cinema. Give examples of expressive devices in the silent film or films you have studied.
- What are the differing purposes of a realist cinema and an expressive cinema?
- Are there examples from the silent film or films you have studied that combine both a realist and an expressive cinema? To what effect?
- Do you agree with Bazin that cinema should aim to show an objective reality? What arguments are there against Bazin's view?

A Level practice question

Discuss how far the silent film or films you have studied are either realist and/or expressionistic.

Answer this question using silent film or films you have studied.

- Set a timer for 30 minutes to practise exam timings.
- Refer to one or two key sequences.
- Look at the mark scheme in the WJEC Eduqas Specimen Assessment Materials (online) and and assess your own work.
- Consider swapping essays with a fellow student and marking each other's response.

Revision activity

Watch a selection of Lumière Brothers and Georges Méliès early short films to increase your understanding of the differences between a realist and an expressive style of cinema.

Knowledge booster

You do not have to 'name-drop' André Bazin as a theorist in the examination. However, it is useful to understand his argument and apply it to the silent film or films you have studied.

Search online for Bazin and realism. There are many good websites which clearly explain his arguments.

Sunrise (Murnau, 1927)

Sunrise exemplifies filmmaking at its artistic peak during the late silent period. Director F. W. Murnau used every device available to filmmakers at the time to produce a lyrical, artistic and timeless love story. *Sight and Sound* magazine voted *Sunrise* the fifth greatest film ever made in their 2017 Greatest Films poll. The film is hailed by critics as a masterpiece. Martin Scorsese described the film as a 'super-production, an experimental film and a visionary poem'.

Revision activity

Read pages 252–253 of the textbook.

Make notes or underline the key features of German Expressionist films. Write down examples from *Sunrise* which exemplify each key feature of German Expressionism.

Activity
Film movements: German Expressionism

Answer the first question below to help you contextualise the film movement of German Expressionism and think about how you might explain it concisely in an introduction.

- How would you describe the German Expressionist movement in three sentences? Use the images below from German Expressionist films to help answer the question

The Cabinet of Dr Caligari (Wiene, 1920)

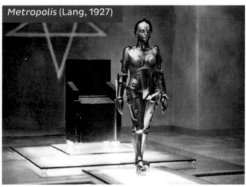

Metropolis (Lang, 1927)

Nosferatu (Murnau, 1922)

- Give a specific example of a moment or sequence in *Sunrise* which best exemplifies the look of German Expressionist films. In three sentences, analyse the use of mise-en-scène, cinematography and editing in the moment or sequence you have chosen.

Revising the specialist areas: the realist and the expressive in *Sunrise*

Sunrise combines elements of German Expressionism and **Kammerspielfilm** and classic Hollywood cinema. Let's revise these three modes in relation to the critical debate of the realist and the expressive.

German Expressionism

- An expressive artistic movement which emerged in Germany in the early 1900s
- Stylistically, expressionist films are characterised by high contrasting and/or harsh lighting to create shadows
- Tilted, disorientating camera angles
- Distorted and stylised studio sets
- Actors may merge with the settings.

Kammerspielfilm – A popular genre in German cinema of the 1920s. They were intimate, realist drama films which focused on characters' inner or domestic lives and explored the psychology of their characters.

Classical Hollywood cinema – A mode of filmmaking developed by Hollywood studios during the 1920s. Hollywood films offered a verisimilitude (a believability or an impression of reality within the filmic world) through linear narratives, a clear sense of cause and effect, and continuity 'invisible' editing.

Activity

Re-watch the opening five minutes of *Sunrise* then answer the following questions:

- Which modes of filmmaking are evident in the sequence (e.g. Expressionism, Kammerspielfilm or classical Hollywood)?
- How does the sequence combine elements of these modes and to what effect?

Knowledge booster

Debates: realist and expressive

Sunrise was produced for Fox, a Hollywood studio, and contains elements of Hollywood cinema of the late silent period. The realism in classical Hollywood cinema is referred to as 'classical Hollywood realism' or the 'classic realist text'. Search these terms online then answer the following question:

How is classical Hollywood realism different from other types of realism (e.g. documentary realism)?

Knowledge booster

Technology and *Sunrise*

Cinematographer John Bailey explains that the opening montage section, 'Vacation Time' was achieved *'in camera on a single strand of film, by masking part of the frame, then rewinding and exposing another section'.*

Revising the contexts of *Sunrise*

Activity

Historical and social contexts and representations of gender

The 1920s was an exciting period in 20th-century history. American women were granted the right to vote in August 1920. It was a period of economic prosperity and the development of American cities. The 1920s '**flapper girl**' personified this era of **urbanisation**, **modernity** and relative freedoms. In *Sunrise*, The Woman from the City can be read as a representation of this modern woman. Look at this image of the Woman from the City and re-watch sequences from *Sunrise* where she appears.

Answer the following questions:

- How does the Woman from the City represent the modern 1920s woman through her dress codes?
- What comment does *Sunrise* make about this urban woman, free from domesticity? Is the film ultimately critical of these changes in women's roles?

Social contexts

Provide a definition for the following terms associated with America and the 1920s:

- Urbanisation
- Modernity
- Flapper girls
- The Jazz Age.

Revision activity

Contexts and *Sunrise*

Search online for Allen and Gomery's chapter on *Sunrise* in *Film History* (available as a PDF).

Answer the following questions:

1. Why did Fox give Murnau complete freedom on *Sunrise*?

2. Why did Fox choose to hire Murnau?

3. What is a 'prestige picture'?

4. How did American critics respond to *Sunrise* when it was first released? Why did American critics respond in this way?

Knowledge booster

Sunrise was the first commercial feature film to use the Fox Movietone sound-on-film system. Search 'Movietone sound-on-film' online. What was revolutionary about these early sound-on-film systems?

Institutional contexts

Answer the following quiz-style questions to test your knowledge of the production and reception of *Sunrise*. You can search for the answers online.

- Why did Fox want to make a German Expressionist film?
- *Sunrise* represents the transition from silent to sound film. What was the name of the first feature-length talkie released in the same year?
- What was the name of the famous German film studio which became known for German Expressionist films in the 1920s?
- Which two Academy Awards did *Sunrise* win in 1929?
- True or False? *Sunrise* was not a financial success on its initial release.

Activity

Revision essay question

Answer the following essay question. Aim to write 300 words.

How has studying the institutional and social contexts of *Sunrise* developed your understanding of the film?

Key sequence analysis : The Man meets The Woman from the City

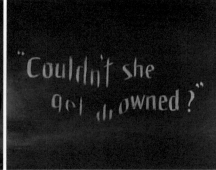

Re-watch the sequence where The Man meets The Woman from the City in the foggy marsh, then write a 500-word analysis focusing on the core and specialist areas. Use the questions below to help structure your analysis.

Film form

- How is lighting used and how does it contribute to the overall mood of this sequence?
- How does the **mise-en-scène** represent the doomed nature of The Man's relationship with The Woman from the City?
- How is **editing** used to help accentuate the differences between The Woman from the City and The Wife?
- What are the binary oppositions presented in the sequence and how are they presented visually?
- How does the **soundtrack** give a sense of foreboding?
- How does The Man's **performance**, as he wades through the marshes, reflect that he is in a nightmarish world?
- What is the purpose of the long tracking shots and how do they contribute to the film's overall **aesthetic**?

Contexts and representations

- How does The Woman from the City **represent** the modern, urban woman?
- How is the film critical of this type of woman? Comment on her costume, hair and make-up and performance.

Revision activity

Read the BFI Classics book on *Sunrise* by Lucy Fischer. Make notes or highlight sections which increase your knowledge and understanding of the film's form, context, representations and use of Expressionism.

Revision activity

Consider how *Sunrise* has elements in common with other Hollywood and Fox films of the era.

Watch sequences from another Fox film starring Janet Gaynor called *Street Angel* (Borzage, 1928). Note down any similarities between this film and *Sunrise*.

Specialist area: Realist and expressive

- Which moments in the sequence are more typical of German Expressionism?
- How are expressive elements used to develop narrative and character?
- What special effects are used in the sequence (e.g. superimposition) and what impact do they have?
- How does the sequence give the audience a sense of The Man's inner psychological turmoil?
- How are intertitles used in an expressionist way?
- How are abstract design, montage and special effects used to represent the city?

Knowledge booster

Special effects and technology in *Sunrise*

For each of the following terms, write a definition then give a specific example of where the effect is used in *Sunrise*:

- Matte painting
- Forced perspective
- Slanted sets and props

You can check your definitions on page 258 of the textbook.

Sample essay on aesthetics in *Sunrise*

Although produced for a Hollywood studio, to a certain extent *Sunrise* (Murnau, 1927) reflects the aesthetic qualities of the German Expressionist movement of the 1920s. German Expressionist art is characterised by a distorted view of reality to create an emotional impact. Key expressionist films such as *The Cabinet of Dr Caligari* and *Metropolis* were successful German productions, replete with the aesthetic qualities of angular and distorted imagery and exaggerated movements of actors. Expressionist films were popular with Hollywood studios, and directors such as Murnau were seen by studios and audiences as artists. As a result, Fox studios gave Murnau creative freedom and a large budget to direct *Sunrise*, enabling the huge constructed sets and special effects typical of expressionist films. The opening montage of the city reflects the aesthetics of expressionism, as images of an artificial city are superimposed to create a collage of expressive images. A poster advertising 'summer time' dissolves into a railway station, created through the use of miniatures. Later in the sequence, a cruise ship is

Introduction demonstrates knowledge and understanding of the film movement

Contextual knowledge applied to a key sequence

overlaid with a cityscape, representing the modern urban city as a place of excitement and a visual spectacle.

Introduces debate by demonstrating how *Sunrise* combines both realist and expressive elements

However, Murnau also draws upon elements of realism in *Sunrise*. His films combine elements of Expressionism with the Kammerspielfilm – these were psychologically realist, intimate dramas which focused on the lives of the working and lower-middle classes. The marsh sequence, where The Man meets The Woman from the City, best exemplifies how Murnau combined the psychological realism of Kammerspielfilm with Expressionism. The dark, muddy marsh, which appears to be lit by moonlight, has both a realistic aesthetic, yet also is symbolic, reflecting the sordid nature of the relationship between The Man and The Woman. The Man imagines himself drowning his wife, presented through a dissolve and a slow static long shot. This subjective reality is typical of Kammerspielfilm, while The Woman's imagining of the city, followed by a montage of city life, is more typical of German Expressionism. The city is represented in an abstract, expressionist manner. Images of the dancers and musicians are expressionistic, as their movements form part of the overall choreographed composition within the frame. Even the title cards are expressive, as 'drowned' drips down off the screen, reflecting the motion of an actual drowning. Here elements of psychological realism and expressionism complement, rather than contradict each other.

Application of the debate to a key sequence

In some regards, *Sunrise* has the tropes of a Hollywood film, particularly in its simple love triangle plot. The affirmation of The Man's love for his Wife presents a conventional ending. Murnau intended the characters to be universal types, known only as The Man, The Wife and The Woman from The City. The Woman and The Wife are presented as binary oppositions. The Woman reflects the modern, urban woman, free from the constraints of marriage – this is represented through her heavy make-up, bobbed hair and dark, tight dress. In contrast, The Wife is presented as homely, rural and motherly. During the marsh sequence, the film cuts between The Woman in the darkly lit marsh and The Wife at home, cradling a baby, with her face fully lit. These two tropes of womanhood were commonplace throughout Hollywood films and also feature in German Expressionist films, as evidenced by robot Maria vs kindly, caring Maria in *Metropolis*.

Awareness of how the film also contains aspects of Hollywood cinema with examples

Short conclusion

Overall, *Sunrise* does reflect some of the aesthetic qualities associated with German Expressionism. However, it combines these with the psychological realism (Kammerspiel) and the conventional Hollywood narrative to create a poetic, artistic film.

Finish it

Complete the following practice 20-mark exam question response on silent film using *Sunrise*. The first short paragraph is written for you. Aim to use one or two key sequences from the film.

Explore how editing and mise-en-scène are used in the silent film or films you have studied.

In *Sunrise*, mise-en-scène is used for both realist and expressive purposes to demonstrate the opposition between city and country, the modern, urban woman and the more domestic, homely wife. At times, long takes rather than quick edits are employed to contribute to the poetic and fluid aesthetic of the film, representing the emotional journey of The Man and The Wife.

The Buster Keaton short films (1920–1922)

We will revise the four Buster Keaton short films, *One Week* (1920), *The Scarecrow* (1920), *The 'High Sign'* (1921) and *Cops* (1922).

We will contextualise the films within 1920s American society and the development of Hollywood cinema. We will then apply the core areas of film form and representations, and the specialist area of the realist and the expressive.

We recommend that you re-watch and revise all four Buster Keaton short films. In the exam, you can focus on one or two relevant sequences from any of the four films which best exemplifies the point you are making. For instance, the opening gag in *Cops* where Keaton is behind bars may be a good sequence to use to discuss how editing and cinematography are used to create a gag.

Activity

Buster Keaton and American silent film comedy

Revise how the short films are examples of gag-based comedy, a genre and movement hugely popular in America during the 1920s. Answer the following questions on silent film comedy to help you contextualise the short films within this movement:

- Why was comedy such a popular genre in the silent era?
- What is slapstick comedy? Give two examples of how slapstick is used in any of the four Buster Keaton short films.
- Who were the other iconic silent film clowns? What were the similarities between them and Keaton?
- Many silent comedians, including Buster Keaton, developed their craft in Vaudeville. What was Vaudeville and how can we see its influence in the Buster Keaton short films?
- Keystone was an important studio for developing silent film comedy and comedians' personas, including Keaton's persona. What was Keystone's 'house style' and what series of films are they most famous for?

Knowledge booster quiz

1. The Keaton shorts are also known as **'two-reelers'**. Why were short films of about 20 minutes called 'two-reelers'?

2. What is an **iris shot**? Give an example of an iris shot from one of the four Keaton short films.

3. What is the name of the female actress who appears as Keaton's young wife in *One Week*?

Knowledge booster

Buster Keaton was influenced by artist Rube Goldberg (1883–1970). Goldberg created cartoon strips featuring invented mechanical devices that would make simple, everyday tasks convoluted.

Look at this example of one of Goldberg's cartoons and search for other examples online.

Find examples in the Buster Keaton shorts which are clearly influenced by these cartoons.

Revision activity

British comedian Paul Merton is an expert on silent film comedy. Search for his book *Silent comedy* and television series *Silent Clowns*, Episode 1: Buster Keaton. This will help you contextualise the Buster Keaton short films within the movement of American silent comedy. You will also learn more about Keaton's childhood and career.

Contextualising Buster Keaton's short films

This activity will help you revise the four Buster Keaton short films within their historical, social, political and institutional contexts.

For each contextual area, give examples from any of the four Buster Keaton short films. The first example is completed for you.

Context		Examples
	Historical, social and cultural: Increased consumerism and advertising	*One Week is based on the Ford Documentary advert Home Made (1919) selling prefabricated homes. In One Week, however, Keaton is unable to construct the perfect home.*
	Historical and social: Urbanisation	
	Political: The suffrage movement	
	Historical and social: Expanding transport systems, e.g. railways	
	Historical and social: The machine age	
	Political: Mistrust of authority figures	
	Institutional: The Hollywood star system	
	Cultural: Art movement of cubism and geometry in American art of the 1920s and 1930s	
	Cultural: Keaton's influence on Surrealism	

Film form and representations

Consider how aspects of film form and representations are used in the four Buster Keaton short films. Give examples from one or two of the short films for each area. The first example is completed for you.

Cinematography ■ Flat lighting ■ Deep focus	Cops: Long-shot of Keaton chased down an alleyway by the cops. Deep focus and flat lighting give perspective and enable the audience to clearly see Keaton outwit the cops by grabbing the moving car in the foreground while the cops fall over each other in the background. Keaton in the centre of the frame keeps the audience focused on him.
Mise-en-scène ■ Objects take on a dual function ■ Fascination with mechanical objects and devices	
Editing ■ Cross-cutting ■ Long takes ■ Edits to create a gag or fool the spectator	
Performance ■ Deadpan expression ■ Exaggerated use of the physical body	
Representations: ■ Defying traditional masculine roles ■ Women as love interests	

The realist and the expressive

Keaton's films combine elements of realism and surrealism to create comedy. Consider how he uses real locations, long takes and deep focus with surreal gags. Re-watch the sequence in *The High Sign* where Keaton is engulfed by the ever-expanding newspaper.

■ How does this sequence combine the realist and the expressive?

■ Find two other examples of this combination of the realist and expressive in any of the four films. How does this combination of the two enhance the comedy?

Sample essay on aesthetics in the Buster Keaton short films

Silent film comedy was a key movement in American cinema of the 1920s, as slapstick and gag-based comedy did not require dialogue and could be easily understood by audiences.

American silent film comedy developed from popular cultural forms such as Vaudeville, where comedians and acrobats would perform to audiences. Keaton developed his craft

A brief, relevant introduction

Applies knowledge of the development of silent film comedy to a key sequence	in Vaudeville as part of a family act, doing comedy acrobatic routines. In *Cops*, Keaton displays his acrobatic skills and death-defying stunts by turning a ladder into a see-saw, running up and down to distribute his weight to outwit the police officers clinging to either side.
Use of film language and focus on aesthetics	When Keaton is chased across the streets of Los Angeles by the entire city police force in *Cops*, we see this in long shot and with a deep focus and flat lighting. These were typical aesthetic devices used to present a chase gag in silent cinema, allowing the audience to focus on the gag and enjoy Keaton's ability to outwit large numbers of bumbling police officers. *Cops* is also typical of American silent film comedy's trend of mocking policemen and distrust of authority figures. This developed from Mack Sennett's Keystone Studios series, Keystone Cops, featuring comedic policemen in comedy chase sequences.
Knowledge of comedy personas applied to a key moment	The American silent film comedians such as Chaplin, Lloyd and Fatty Arbuckle developed unique personas through costume, physique and performance, which formed the overall aesthetic of their films. Keaton was known as the Great Stone Face, a persona he developed in Vaudeville when he noticed that audiences laughed more when he stayed completely expressionless. For instance, in *One Week*, when the train destroys his flat-pack home, the camera cuts to a medium close-up of Keaton's expressionless face which heightens the gag. Keaton was often represented as the 'little man', using his short and thin physique to depict a man who is overwhelmed by the forces of nature. This persona contributes to the overall aesthetic of 'the little man vs the modern world' in his films.
Detailed key sequence analysis	In *One Week*, Keaton battles against the elements to build the flat-pack house yet fails as it appears the house and the elements such as a hurricane conspire against him, shown in long-shot as the house, placed on a giant turntable, turns faster as Keaton appears tiny in the frame, clinging on to the side of the house. The house eventually takes on a surreal cubist form and appears to form a face, a reference to the cultural artistic movement of cubism where artists such as Picasso created fragmented and abstract shapes.
Application of knowledge to another Keaton short film	There was a fascination in American silent comedy with gadgets and the machine age. In *The Scarecrow*, all objects in Keaton's home have a duel function for comedic effect. For instance, the gramophone player cleverly functions as an oven. The house is full of contraptions, a reference to the comic illustrations of Rube Goldberg which depicted mechanical inventions that made simple jobs complicated.
A short conclusion	The clever use of gadgets or contraptions within the mise-en-scène forms part of the overall aesthetic of Keaton's films. Overall, these four Keaton shorts reflect the aesthetic qualities of American silent film comedy, with physical gags, devices such as deep-focus, flat lighting and static cameras and a fascination with machinery.

Finish it

Complete the following practice 20-mark exam question response on the four Buster Keaton short films. The first short paragraph is written for you. Aim to use one or two key sequences from any of the four films.

Explore how editing and mise-en-scène are used in the silent film or films you have studied.

Editing and mise-en-scène are used in the four Buster Keaton shorts to accentuate the visual comedy and create symmetrical, ingenious imagery. Keaton's performance is integral to the mise-en-scène, often centring himself in the frame as objects or the natural world around him appear to conspire against him.

Film movements: Experimental film

What to revise

The core areas:

- **Film form**: cinematography, mise-en-scène, sound, editing and performance
- **Representations** and **aesthetics**
- Social, cultural, political, historical and institutional (including production) **contexts**.

The specialist areas:

- **Narrative**
- **Auteur.**

How you will be assessed at A Level

- You choose one essay question from a choice of two
- The question is worth **20 marks**.

How to approach a 20-mark question on experimental film

- We recommend that you spend 30 minutes maximum answering the question.
- This is a fairly short essay. Keep to the point and only include analysis that is relevant to the question.
- You only need to provide a very short introduction and conclusion.
- Focus on one or two sequences from the experimental film option you have studied in detail.
- Look at the sample annotated response on page 145.

We will revise the film movements associated with the experimental film option you have studied, then revise the specialist areas of narrative and auteur. These activities can be applied to any of the experimental film option you have studied. We will then revise *Daises* and *Pulp Fiction* as case studies.

Revising film movements and experimental film

Each of the experimental films on the specification is an example of an experimental film movement. These are:

- 1990s **postmodernism** and Hollywood Indie cinema: *Pulp Fiction*
- 1990s postmodernism and Hong Kong New Wave: *Fallen Angels*
- 1990s postmodernism and Digital cinema: *Timecode*
- European **Avant-garde** and French New Wave: *Vivre sa vie*
- European Avant-garde and Czech New Wave: *Daisies* and European Avant-garde: *Saute ma ville*.

Activity

Search online for the WJEC Eduqas Film Movement Study Guides for resources on film movements. Then create a poster explaining and defining the experimental film movement you have studied. Include:

- The key characteristics of the film movement, including the formal and stylistic innovations of the movement.

- The social, political, cultural and institutional contexts of the film movement.
- Quotes from any related manifestos/critical writing associated with the movement.
- Key auteurs and films associated with the film movement.
- Annotated stills from the film you have studied which best exemplify the characteristics of the film movement.

Revising the specialist area of narrative in experimental film

Key points:

- The focus in this section is on **narrative experimentation**.
- Consider how the experimental film option you have studied experiment with narrative through the overall narrative structure and through key elements of film form (e.g. editing, mise-en-scène, sound, etc.).
- Consider how the experimental film option you have studied may offer more complex characterisations and representations than those in mainstream narrative films.

Revision activity

Think about your response as a spectator when you first watched the experimental film you studied. Answer the following questions:

1. What seemed unfamiliar and strange about the film?

2. In what ways does the film challenge you?

Activity

You have studied more conventional narrative structures in Component 1, Section C: British cinema. Choose one of the British films you have studied. Complete the table at the bottom of this page comparing the narrative devices used in the British film and experimental film you have studied. This will help you understand the differences between conventional and experimental narratives.

Here is an example to help you which compares *Shaun of the Dead* and *Pulp Fiction*:

Narrative device	British film	Experimental film
	Shaun of the Dead	*Pulp Fiction*
Plot and story order	Linear narrative and 3-act structure.	Edited out of story order. The spectator must piece together the narrative.
Narrative and characters associated with genre conventions	Hybrid of comedy and zombie horror films. Shaun is the 'everyman' who becomes heroic.	Overturns genre conventions; e.g. we see hitmen Jules and Vince in the build-up to a job having ordinary conversations.

Now complete the table using the films you have studied:

Narrative device	British film	Experimental film
Plot and story order		
Genre conventions		
Key character functions		

Use of editing, e.g. continuity/discontinuity		
Key messages and ideologies communicated through narrative resolution		

Activity

Experimental films as art cinema

David Bordwell defines art cinema as having the following characteristics (*Art Cinema as a Mode of Practice*, 1979):

- A realistic cinema with use of real locations.
- Narratives are explicitly against the **classical Hollywood narrative** mode. Looser narratives and looser sense of cause and effect. Narratives have a drifting, episodic quality.
- Psychologically complex characters dealing with real problems.
- Characters may lack defined desires and goals.
- A cinema of reaction rather than action – focus on psychological effects and their causes.
- May have a documentary factuality and/or an intense psychological subjectivity.
- Violations of classical film time and space, e.g. jump-cuts, plot manipulations of story order.
- Stylistic devices such as the long take, the moving camera and deep focus may be employed.
- Foregrounding of the film's author /auteur – director has creative freedom.
- The viewer expects stylistic signatures rather than order in the narrative.
- Viewers encounter the film and auteur through film festivals, essays, reviews, film education.
- Auteur signatures manifest through violations of classical cinema.
- An ambiguous cinema, reflecting character ambiguity, the author's signature and life's untidiness.

Apply these characteristics to the experimental film option you have studied. How many of them apply? Give specific examples from the experimental film option you have studied.

Revising auteur and experimental film

We have revised definitions of auteur in the Hollywood comparison section on page 34.

In relation to experimental film and auteur, the specification says:

'*This approach sees filmmakers as creative decision makers, responsible for the selection and construction process in films which experiment with narrative and film form.*
    Learners should consider what 'signatures' can be identified for a film as a result of a more experimental approach to the filmmaking process.'

For experimental film, it is accepted that the director-auteur is the creative force, with artistic freedom to direct a more challenging, experimental film. We should remember, however, that film is a collaborative medium and that artistic experimental directors may work closely with key collaborators (e.g. director Wong Kar-wai and cinematographer Christopher Doyle).

Revision activity

Research the distribution and exhibition of the experimental film you have studied.

Answer the following questions:

1. Which companies distributed the film? Are they associated with more independent and experimental films?

2. Where was the film first exhibited? Was it exhibited in mainstream or independent/art-house cinemas?

3. Who are the main target audience for the film? Is this different from the target audiences for mainstream films?

Research the auteur-director of the experimental film option you have studied. Read and watch interviews with the director and watch sequences from their notable films. Answer the following questions using bullet points:

- What are the director's main auteur trademarks?
- What are some of the director's other notable films?
- What are the director's key motivations when making experimental films?
- Who does the director collaborate with (e.g. actors, editor, cinematographer)?
- What do key collaborators contribute to the overall aesthetic of the film option you have studied?

A Level practice question

Explore how far the experimental film option you have studied are experimental in challenging conventional approaches to narrative.

- Set a timer for 30 minutes to practise exam timings.
- Refer to one or two key sequences.
- Provide a very short introduction and conclusion.
- Address the 'how far' element of the question – e.g. you may argue that the film is very experimental or that the film is only experimental to a certain extent.
- Look at the assessment objectives and mark schemes in the Sample Assessment Materials (online) and assess your own work.
- Consider swapping essays with a fellow student and marking each other's response.

Revision tip:

You are not expected to know or reference all of the other films directed by the experimental auteur you have studied. Instead, watch a few sequences from other films to give you a sense of their auteur signature style. In the exam, focus on the film you have studied rather than comparisons to their other films.

Case study 1

Daisies (Chytilová, 1966) and *Saute ma ville* (Akerman, 1969)

Revising the core and specialist areas of *Daisies*

Activity

Key sequence analysis: the opening sequences

We will revise how *Daises* uses elements of film form in experimental ways by analysing the opening sequences. Re-watch the opening three minutes of the film after the title sequence, then annotate the stills below. Use the bullet points to guide your analysis:

	■ Dialogue: The two Maries' view of the world 'gone bad' ■ Sound effects: surreal use of sound ■ Impact of the lack of close-ups
	■ Experimental use of juxtaposition: archive footage of a building collapsing
	■ Move from black and white to colour ■ Use of a match-cut ■ Use of non-naturalistic performance style
	■ The significance of the fruit tree ■ Recurrent motifs of eating and food

Revision activity

Search online for the essay 'Pearls of the Czech New Wave' by Michael Koresky on the *Criterion Collection* website. Go to the section titled 'Daisies: Flower Girls'. Read this section then answer the following questions:

1. Why is Věra Chytilová described as an unconventional filmmaker?

2. What are some of the ways in which the two Maries have been interpreted?

Activity

Revising representations of gender and age

Read film scholar Sarah Griffith's comment on gender representations in *Daisies*:

> '*Due to the ambiguous narrative created by the experimental structure,* Daisies *is able to have two female characters who do not conform to traditional gender roles. Chytilová plays with the expectations of women as constructed by a patriarchal society.*'
> (Screen Culture Online, 2017)

Use this quotation and your own analysis of the film to answer the following questions on representations in *Daisies*. Give examples from the film to illustrate your points.

We're really happy!

- How do the two Maries defy gender stereotypes and expectations of young women?
- How does the film represent women trying to react against a patriarchal society?
- How are the men they date represented in the film?
- How do Marie 1 and Marie 2 defy the male gaze?

Revising the contexts of *Daisies*

Revision activity

Daisies was produced at the time of the second wave of feminism. Research second wave feminism and answer the following questions:

1. When did second wave feminism begin?

2. How did second wave feminism differ from first wave feminism?

3. What were the main ideals and beliefs of second wave feminism?

4. How does *Daisies* reflect second wave feminism?

Activity

Cultural contexts: the Czech New Wave

On YouTube, search for the video essay 'Freedom! Wonder! War! – The Czech New Wave' on the Film Qualia channel.

Watch sequences from other notable Czech New Wave films mentioned in the video essay.

Use the video essay, sequences and your own class notes to create a 15-minute PowerPoint presentation explaining the Czech New Wave. Use annotated stills from Czech New Wave films and images of key directors. Include:

- The political contexts which led to the emergence of Czech New Wave films.
- Czech cinema as a cinema of rebellion, oppositions and a desire for freedom.
- How Czech New Wave directors use allegory (a metaphor used to deliver a broader meaning) and experimental devices to critique the restrictive socialist government.
- The key filmmakers and films of the Czech New Wave.
- The importance of the Prague Film School.

Activity

Social and political contexts: the Prague Spring

Watch the video essay 'The Cold War: The Prague Spring 1968 and the Crisis in Czechoslovakia' on the I'm Stuck – GCSE and A Level Revision YouTube Channel. Read the BBC GCSE Bitesize webpage on the Prague Spring.

Create a visual poster describing Czechoslovakia of the late 1960s and the events of the Prague Spring. Use annotated images and maps of Czechoslovakia. Include:

- The key dates and events that led to the Prague Spring.
- Czechoslovakia under Communist rule.
- The brief flourishing of artistic freedom.
- The Soviet invasion and the end of the Prague Spring.

Revising the specialist area of narrative and *Daisies*

Activity

Claire Clouzot comments on the narrative of *Daisies* that '*there is no involvement, no conventional chronology, no psychological development … no narration*' (*Film Quarterly*, Spring 1968).

Write a 300-word argument explaining how and why *Daisies* has an experimental narrative. Include:

- How experimental narrative devices are used to convey the messages of the film.
- How the experimental narrative challenges the spectator.
- How the experimental narrative offers more complex representations of gender and age.

Activity

Narrative devices and film form

Give examples of how the following five elements of film form are used in experimental ways in *Daisies*. Provide three examples from the film to illustrate your points. The first example is done for you:

Area of film form	Experimental uses in *Daisies*
Sound	*Opening sequence – use of creaking and squeaking sounds when Marie 1 and Marie 2 move. Shows how women are controlled. They want to break free of this.*
Editing	
Mise-en-scène	
Cinematography	
Performance	

Revising the specialist area of auteur in *Daisies*

Activity

Research the life and work of Věra Chytilová. We recommend starting with the article 'Věra Chytilová for Beginners' by Carmen Gray on the BFI website.

Plan a five-minute short documentary summarising Chytilová's auteur signature style, with clips and images from her most notable films. Include all the following descriptors of Věra Chytilová's auteur signature from the textbook:

- Feminist
- Philosophical
- Experimental
- Artistic and aesthetic freedom.

Saute ma ville (Akerman, 1968)

Activity

Write or record an audio commentary for the film, commenting on the core areas and specialist areas of narrative and auteur. Use the bullet points below to help you write the commentary:

- How Akerman comments on domestic drudgery for women.
- The recurrent motifs of entrapment.
- Why Akerman deliberately defies mainstream narrative conventions.
- Use of jump-cuts and lack of continuity.
- Handheld camerawork and long-shots.
- Jarring and asynchronous sound effects.
- Anti-realist performance style.

Pulp Fiction (Tarantino, 1994)

Revising cultural contexts and the film movement of 1990s postmodernism

Pulp Fiction may no longer appear experimental today, as Tarantino is now one of Hollywood's most famous contemporary auteurs. You should therefore contextualise *Pulp Fiction* as experimental for the time period of the 1990s when postmodern film flourished.

Activity

Create an eight-slide PowerPoint presentation explaining postmodernism. Include:

Slide 1: Some common definitions of postmodernism

Slide 2: What was modernism?

Slide 3: What led to postmodernism?

Slide 4: Different aspects of postmodernism

Slide 5: Postmodern cinema

Slides 6–8: Examples of how *Pulp Fiction* exemplifies postmodern cinema.

Activity

Give a definition of each of these aspects of postmodern culture. Provide an example for each one from *Pulp Fiction*. The first example is completed for you.

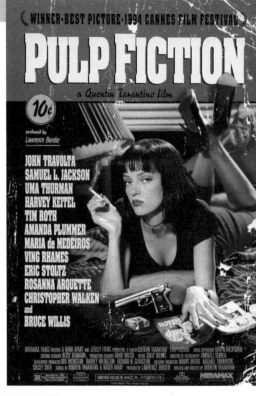

Aspect of postmodernism	Definition	Example from *Pulp Fiction*
Intertextuality	When one media text or film directly references other media texts.	In Jack Rabbit Slims there is a Marylin Monroe look-a-like mimicking a famous scene from one of Monroe's best known films, The Seven Year Itch.
Homage		
Parody		
Self-reflexivity		
Fragmentation		
Irony		

Revision activity

Film reviewer James Woods wrote this harsh critique of *Pulp Fiction*:

'Tarantino represents the final triumph of postmodernism, which is to empty the artwork of all content, thus avoiding its capacity to do anything except helplessly represent our agonies ...
Only in this age could a writer as talented as Tarantino produce artworks so vacuous, so entirely stripped of any politics, metaphysics, or moral interest.' (Guardian 12 November 1994)

Give one argument for and one against this critique using examples from the film to illustrate your points.

Playfulness		
Bridging the gap between high and low culture		

Activity

Re-watch the Jack Rabbit Slims sequence of *Pulp Fiction*. It is loaded with cultural references. How many can you spot?

Now watch the dance sequence from *Band à part* (Godard, 1964). Note the comparisons between this scene and Mia and Vince's dance.

Revising representations in *Pulp Fiction*

Activity
Representations of gender

Re-watch the following sequences:

- Vince arrives at Mia's apartment
- Vince and Mia return to her apartment
- Mia overdoses.

Revision activity

Watch the section of the *Mark Cousins: The Story of Film* documentary on postmodern films of the 1990s. Answer the following questions:

1. How does Cousins define postmodern cinema?

2. How did postmodern cinema offer a break from the mainstream?

3. Who were some of the influential directors and films associated with postmodern cinema?

Write a 400-word analysis on how **gender** is represented in these sequences. Use the bullet points below to help guide your analysis:

- How Mia 'directs' Vince through her instructions over the intercom
- Use of close-ups on Mia's lips and feet
- How Vince rescues Mia after the overdose.

Activity

Representations of ethnicity

Director Spike Lee criticised Tarantino for the excessive use of racially charged language in his films. In 1997, Lee criticised Tarantino's use of the n-word. He said: *'I'm not against the word … and I use it, but Quentin is infatuated with the word. What does he want? To be made an honorary black man? I want Quentin to know that all African-Americans do not think that word is trendy or slick.'*

Tarantino responded: *'As a writer, I demand the right to write any character in the world that I want to write. And to say that I can't do that because I'm white … that is racist.'*

Search online for critics' responses to representations of black Americans and the use of racial language in *Pulp Fiction*, then answer the following questions:

- Why do some critics find Tarantino's use of racial language problematic?
- What arguments do Tarantino and his supporters make against such criticisms?
- Some critics have argued that *Pulp Fiction* is progressive in its representations, creating complex and layered characters. Do you agree with this argument? Give reasons for your answer.

Revising the institutional contexts of *Pulp Fiction*

Pulp Fiction was Miramax's first major production after being bought out by Disney. The film grossed $107.93 million at the US box office.

Pulp Fiction was an example of how more experimental American films can cross over into the mainstream. Such films have been labelled by critics as '**Indiewood** films', as they combine elements of mainstream and Independent.

Activity

Complete the Venn diagram with the conventions of Independent and Hollywood cinema and the crossover between the two:

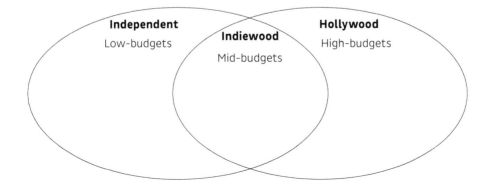

Independent
Low-budgets

Indiewood
Mid-budgets

Hollywood
High-budgets

Revising the narrative of *Pulp Fiction*

Activity

On coloured sticky notes, list the key events in *Pulp Fiction*. List each key event on one sticky note. Then organise the key events in the order they are presented to us. Now re-order the sticky notes, placing each event in story order. Answer the following questions:

- How conventional is the narrative structure of *Pulp Fiction* when placed in story order?
- What is the impact of placing events out of story order? Think about how it challenges you as a spectator.

Key sequence analysis: the opening sequences

Re-watch the opening sequences of *Pulp Fiction*, including Vince and Jules' conversation while they are waiting outside the apartment. Make notes on the **core and specialist areas**. Use the bullet points below to help to guide your analysis.

Core areas

Editing

- Use of long takes
- Freeze-frame.

Mise-en-scène

- Use of costume – Vince and Jules as hitmen
- Pumpkin and Hunny Bunnys' casual attire
- Difficulty placing the film in a specific time period.

Sound

- Blurring of diegetic and non-diegetic sound
- Importance of the musical soundtrack
- Use of everyday conversation not usually seen in films.

Cinematography

- Use of wide shots.

Performance

- Hunny Bunny – the shift from likeable to violent
- Jules and Vince – realistic performances.

Aesthetics

- Hyperreality
- A non-specific time period
- Los Angeles setting.

Representations

- Vince and Jules as atypical hitmen
- Hunny Bunny breaking out of the stereotype with her violent outburst.

Cultural contexts

- Similarities to French New Wave films
- Cultural references and intertextuality.

Institutional contexts

- Indiewood.

Specialist areas

Specialist area of narrative

- Comparison to the film's ending where we see the same events from the perspective of Jules
- Use of the episodic narrative structure
- Humanising of stock genre characters
- Long scenes building up characterisation
- How we think about the scene on second viewing knowing the outcome.

Specialist area of auteur

- Tarantino's auteur signature, including: cultural references, stylised dialogue, and the importance of the soundtrack.

Sample essay on the experimental narrative of *Pulp Fiction*

Pulp Fiction (Tarantino, 1994) is typical of the cultural movement of postmodernism prevalent in Western culture during the 1990s. Indeed, *Pulp Fiction* was the signature postmodern film of the era. It exemplifies the style and ethos of American late capitalism and globalisation, addressing an audience versed in decades of pop culture through cinema, television and popular music. It reflects a period in American cinema of the 1990s which became more playful, self-reflexive and 'knowing' in regard to narrative.

Pulp Fiction's homage to French New Wave of the late 1950s, through the use of long takes, non-heroic characters and playful references throughout, exemplifies this trend of postmodern 'indie' style cinema, which broke down distinctions between high and low culture. The sudden shifts from long takes of long scenes of dialogue to extreme violence were commonplace in French New Wave cinema. *Pulp Fiction* replicates this characteristic of French New Wave throughout. One such example is the opening sequence where 'Pumpkin' and 'Honey Bunny' discuss a hold-up at length, with extensive use of long-shots, then launch into the violent act which is halted through a freeze-frame, another stylistic device used in French New Wave cinema.

Knowledge of the influence of French New Wave with an example from the film

Postmodern narratives often depend on intertextual references which provide pleasure for the spectator. The mise-en-scène in the Jack Rabbit Slims diner evokes a nostalgic 1950s, as live performers do impressions of iconic fifties stars, including Marilyn Monroe. A tracking shot follows behind Vince as he walks through the diner, filled with B-movie film posters. This reflects the postmodern trend for a nostalgia for a mythic past, one the spectator may only be aware of through popular culture. Indeed, *Pulp Fiction*'s soundtrack is a mixture of popular songs from the 1950s to the 1990s, giving the film its ahistorical, nostalgic postmodern feel. *Pulp Fiction* reflects postmodernism's layered referencing, as characters' personalities, clothes, dialogue and even hairstyles are a collage of references. Mia, with her short-bobbed hair, may remind the spectator of Louise Brooks or Anna Karina, or possibly both. Tarantino's use of iconic stars from previous decades, invites spectators to make cultural connections between *Pulp Fiction* and other films. The sequence where Mia and Vince dance at Jack Rabbit Slims diner would remind an audience familiar with *Saturday Night Fever* of Travolta's role in that film. It is also based on the dance sequence in the French New Wave film *Band à part* (1964), yet another layered reference.

Detailed sequence analysis

Links to characterisation

Tarantino experiments with narrative structure by presenting the film out of chronological order. This reflects the trend in postmodern culture to assume an active spectatorship, who can piece together the story themselves. Certain enigmas are never resolved, including what is contained in the briefcase. We only see the briefcase from the point of view of characters such as Vince looking in. This allows spectators to create their own hypothesis and engage in the playful nature of postmodern narratives. Certain sequences also feel like 'off set' discussions, as characters have seemingly banal conversations before they 'perform' their role. This is best exemplified when Vince and Jules discuss foot massages before they enter the apartment and perform their role as hitmen. Such sequences remind us of the performative and constructed nature of film; another postmodern trope, where the audience are constantly reminded that they are watching a fictional construct.

Overall, *Pulp Fiction* reflects and exemplifies postmodern narratives of the 1990s. Indeed, the film set the trend for a plethora of postmodern films commonplace in American cinema of the 1990s.

Finish it

Complete the following practice 20-mark exam question response on experimental film, using *Pulp Fiction*. The first short paragraph is written for you. Aim to use at least one key sequence from the film.

Explore how two aspects of film form (e.g. mise-en-scène, cinematography, sound, editing, performance) contribute to the experimental identity of the film you have studied.

In *Pulp Fiction*, editing and performance are used in self-referential ways to contribute to the postmodern, experimental identity of a film layered with cinematic references. The film is deliberately edited out of story order, encouraging an active spectator to piece together the narrative in the 'correct' order. The performances in the film alternate between realistic and heavily stylised.

A Level Film Studies revision checklist

Here is a brief overview of what you need to revise for your forthcoming A Level Film Studies examinations. You can tick off each area once you feel confident that you have revised it.

Hollywood 1930–1990 (comparative study)

You have studied one film from group 1 and one film from group 2:

Group 1: Classical Hollywood

Casablanca (Curtiz, 1942)

The Lady from Shanghai (Welles, 1947)

Johnny Guitar (Ray, 1954)

Vertigo (Hitchcock, 1958)

Some Like it Hot (Wilder, 1959)

Group 2: New Hollywood

Bonnie and Clyde (Penn, 1967)

One Flew Over the Cuckoo's Nest (Forman, 1975)

Apocalypse Now (Coppola, 1979)

Blade Runner (Scott, 1982)

Do the Right Thing (Lee, 1989)

What to revise	Group 1 film	Group 2 film
Core areas: Film form		
Core areas: Aesthetics		
Core areas: Representations of age, gender and ethnicity		
Core areas: Political, social, cultural and institutional contexts		
Specialist area: auteur		

American film since 2005 (two-film study)

You have studied one film from group 1 and one film from group 2:

Group 1: Mainstream film

No Country for Old Men (Coen Brothers, 2007)

Inception (Nolan, 2010)

Selma (Duvernay, 2013)

Carol (Haynes, 2015)

La La Land (Chazelle, 2016).

Group 2: Contemporary independent film

Winter's Bone (Granik, 2010)

Frances Ha (Baumbach, 2012)

Beasts of the Southern Wild (Zeitlin, 2012)

Boyhood (Linklater, 2015)

Captain Fantastic (Ross, 2015)

What to revise	Group 1 film	Group 2 film
Core areas: Film form		
Core areas: Aesthetics		
Core areas: Representations of age, gender and ethnicity		
Core areas: Political, social, cultural and institutional contexts		
Specialist area: Spectatorship		
Specialist area: Ideology		

Component 1, Section C

British film since 1995 (two-film study)

You have studied two films from this list:

Secrets and Lies (Leigh, 1996)

Trainspotting (Boyle, 1996)

Sweet Sixteen (Loach, 2002)

Shaun of the Dead (Wright, 2004)

This is England (Meadows, 2006)

Moon (Jones, 2009)

Fish Tank (Arnold, 2009)

We need to Talk about Kevin (Ramsay, 2011)

Sightseers (Wheatley, 2012)

Under the Skin (Glazer, 2013)

What to revise	Film 1	Film 2
Core areas: Film form		
Core areas: Aesthetics		
Core areas: Representations of age, gender and ethnicity		
Core areas: Political, social, cultural and institutional contexts		
Specialist area: Narrative		
Specialist area: Ideology		

Component 2, Section A

Global film (two-film study):

You have studied one film from group 1 and one film from group 2:

Group 1: European film:

Life is Beautiful (Benigni, Italy, 1997)

Pan's Labyrinth (Del Toro, Spain, 2006)

The Diving Bell and the Butterfly (Schnabel France, 2007)

Ida (Pawlikowski, Poland, 2013)

Mustang (Ergűnez, France/Turkey, 2015)

Victora (Schipper, Germany, 2015)

Group 2: Outside Europe:

Dil Se (Ratnam, India, 1998)

City of God (Mereilles, Brazil, 2002)

House of Flying Daggers (Zhang, China, 2004)

Timbuktu (Sissako, Mauritania, 2014)

Wild Tales (Szifrón, Argentina, 2014)

Taxi Tehran (Panahi, Iran, 2015)

What to revise	group 1 film	Group 2 film
Core areas: Film form		
Core areas: Aesthetics		
Core areas: Representations of age, gender and ethnicity		
Core areas: Political, social, cultural and institutional contexts		

Component 2, Section B

Documentary film

You have studied one of the following films:

- *Sisters in Law* (Ayisi/Longinotto, Cameroon/UK, 2005)
- *The Arbor* (Barnard, UK, 2010)
- *Stories We Tell* (Polley, Canada, 2012)
- *20,000 Days on Earth* (Forsyth / Pollard, UK, 2014)
- *Amy* (Kapadia, UK, 2015)

What to revise	Documentary film
Core areas: Film form	
Core areas: Aesthetics	
Core areas: Representations of age, gender and ethnicity	
Core areas: Political, social, cultural and institutional contexts	
Specialist area: Filmmakers' theories	
Specialist area: Critical debates: The significance of digital technology in film	

Component 2, Section C
Silent cinema

You have studied one of the following film options:

- *Keaton shorts – One Week* (1920), *The Scarecrow* (1920), *The 'High Sign'* (1921) and *Cops* (1922)
- *Strike* (Eisenstein, USSR, 1924)
- *Man With a Movie Camera* (Vertov, USSR, 1929) and *À Propos de Nice* (Vigo, 1930)
- *Sunrise* (Murnau, US, 1927)
- *Spies* (Lang, Germany, 1928).

What to revise	Silent film option
Core areas: Film form	
Core areas: Aesthetics	
Core areas: Representations of age, gender and ethnicity	
Core areas: Political, social, cultural and institutional contexts	
Specialist area: Critical debates: The realist and the expressive	

Component 2, Section D
Experimental film

You have studied one of the following film options:

- *Vivre sa vie* (Godard, France, 1962)
- *Daisies* (Chytilova, Czechoslovakia, 1965) and Saute ma ville (Akerman, Belgium, 1968)
- *Pulp Fiction* (Tarantino, US, 1994)
- *Fallen Angels* (Wong, Hong Kong, 1995)
- *Timecode* (Figgis, US, 2000)

What to revise	Experimental film option
Core areas: Film form	
Core areas: Aesthetics	
Core areas: Representations of age, gender and ethnicity	
Core areas: Political, social, cultural and institutional contexts	
Specialist area: Auteur	
Specialist area: Narrative	

AS Level Film Studies revision checklist

Here is a brief overview of what you need to revise for your forthcoming AS Level Film Studies examinations. You can tick off each area once you feel confident that you have revised it.

Hollywood 1930–1990 (comparative study)

You have studied one film from group 1 and one film from group 2:

Group 1: Classical Hollywood

Casablanca (Curtiz, 1942)

The Lady from Shanghai (Welles, 1947)

Johnny Guitar (Ray, 1954)

Vertigo (Hitchcock, 1958)

Some Like it Hot (Wilder, 1959)

Group 2: New Hollywood

Bonnie and Clyde (Penn, 1967)

One Flew Over the Cuckoo's Nest (Forman, 1975)

Apocalypse Now (Coppola, 1979)

Blade Runner (Scott, 1982)

Do the Right Thing (Lee, 1989)

What to revise	Group 1 film	Group 2 film
Core areas: Film form		
Core areas: Aesthetics		
Core areas: Representations of age, gender and ethnicity		
Core areas: Political, social, cultural and institutional contexts		

Contemporary American independent film

You have studied one of the following contemporary American independent films:

- *Winter's Bone* (Granik, 2010)
- *Frances Ha* (Baumbach, 2012)
- *Beasts of the Southern Wild* (Zeitlin, 2012)
- *Boyhood* (Linklater, 2015)
- *Captain Fantastic* (Ross, 2015)

What to revise	Film
Core areas: Film form	
Core areas: Aesthetics	
Core areas: Representations of age, gender and ethnicity	
Core areas: Political, social, cultural and institutional contexts	
Specialist area: Spectatorship	

Component 2, Section A
British film since 1995 (two-film study)

You have studied two films from this list:

Secrets and Lies (Leigh, 1996)

Trainspotting (Boyle, 1996)

Sweet Sixteen (Loach, 2002)

Shaun of the Dead (Wright, 2004)

This is England (Meadows, 2006)

Moon (Jones, 2009)

Fish Tank (Arnold, 2009)

We Need to Talk about Kevin (Ramsay, 2011)

Sightseers (Wheatley, 2012)

Under the Skin (Glazer, 2013)

What to revise	Film 1	Film 2
Core areas: Film form		
Core areas: Aesthetics		
Core areas: Representations of age, gender and ethnicity		
Core areas: Political, social, cultural and institutional contexts		
Specialist area: Narrative		

Component 2, Section B
Non-English language European film

You have studied one of the following non-English language European films:

Group 1: European film

- *Life is Beautiful* (Benigni, Italy, 1997)
- *Pan's Labyrinth* (Del Toro, Spain, 2006)
- *The Diving Bell and the Butterfly* (Schnabel, France, 2007)
- *Ida* (Pawlikowski, Poland, 2013)
- *Mustang* (Ergünez, France/Turkey, 2015)
- *Victoria* (Schipper, Germany, 2015)

What to revise	Film
Core areas: Film form	
Core areas: Aesthetics	
Core areas: Representations of age, gender and ethnicity	
Core areas: Political, social, cultural and institutional contexts	

Glossary

Aesthetic

The style adopted by an artist (in a film's case the filmmaker) or a film movement. For example, despite the different settings of *Trainspotting* (Boyle, 1996) and *Slumdog Millionaire* (Boyle, 2009), both films share a visual look and feel created by the director's (Danny Boyle) high-energy visual style, by way of his choice of camerawork, editing and music.

Allegory

A story or images with a meaning or messages about particular issues or concerns, usually associated with politics, religion or morals. By representing abstract messages through narrative, characters or images, they can be more understandable. Allegory can also be used to hide a film's explicit meaning, particularly if a film is made in a country with a repressive political regime.

Alignment

Spectator alignment refers to how a film may position us with a particular character to encourage us to identify with that character.

Auteur

The filmmaker has enough influence on a film that they are the author of the film. They may have a particular trademark or signature recognisable across a body of work. The term is usually ascribed to the director, although other key creative influential talent, such as an editor or cinematographer, can also be an auteur.

Avant-garde films

Films that are artistic, experimental and challenge mainstream conventions. They are often non-narrative films made outside of a major studio. Avant-garde cinema is usually associated with European artistic filmmakers, although there are examples of avant-garde films and filmmakers in other cinemas outside Europe.

Binary opposition

When two characters or ideologies are set up against one another. It is an important concept of structuralism and can be used to structure representations and help create meaning.

Cinéma vérité

A style of documentary filmmaking, also called observational cinema.

CinemaScope

A widescreen format developed by 20th Century Fox. When projected onto the cinema screen, the width is two and a half times its height. CinemaScope was used in certain Hollywood films from 1953 until the late 1960s.

Cinematographer

Responsible for the look of the film; in charge of the camera technique and translates the director's vision onto the screen, advising the director on camera angles, lighting and special effects.

Classical Hollywood narrative

The predominant narrative style and structure of Hollywood cinema from the late 1910s to the 1960s. It is characterised by linear, cause and effect narratives, protagonists with a defined goal and narrative closure.

Contexts

The factors, situations and conditions that surround a film, essential for understanding why the film looks the way it does, its themes, issues, messages and values.

Continuity editing

The predominant style of editing in narrative film. The edits should create a logical coherence and continuous narrative action. The shots should flow seamlessly and not confuse the audience. Conventions of continuity editing include the use of shot/reverse shot, the 180-degree rule and match-on-action.

Ethnicity

Social groups with a shared common homeland, language, culture, traditions and religion.

European art-house

Attributed to European movements and filmmakers after World War II, including French New Wave and directors such as Federico Fellini. European art-house narratives are less motivated by cause and effect and tend to have more ambiguous characters and drifting, episodic narratives. Stylistically, they often defy Classical Hollywood stylistic conventions with more experimental filmic devices.

Expressionist

Expressionist films depict a widely distorted reality for emotional effect.

Feminism

Social and political movements which advocate for equal rights for women. Feminist movements take many forms, including liberal feminism and radical feminism. In the West, there have been three waves of feminism. First wave feminism (late 19th to early 20th century) was the suffrage movement, fighting for voting rights for women. The second wave (late 1960s to 1980s) focused on discrimination and how the personal lives of women were bound by oppressive patriarchal structures. The third wave (1990s to date) is an intersectional and international feminism.

Filmmakers' theories

A filmmaker's approach to making a film. In A Level Film Studies, you will study the approaches of one or two documentary filmmakers for the specialist area filmmakers' theories.

Formalism

Looks at a film's structure and recognises the differences between the story and how it is told through the plot. This includes a focus on the formal elements of a film.

French New Wave

A movement in French cinema of the late 1950s and early 1960s. Directors, such as Jacques Demy, Agnès Varda, Alain Resnais, Claude Chabrol, Jean-Luc Godard and François Truffaut, created stylish, energetic and self-conscious films. French New Wave films were typified by on-location shooting, naturalistic acting and ambiguous or unresolved endings. While new wave directors were inspired by Hollywood auteurs such as Hitchcock, they often broke the rules of Classical Hollywood films. For instance, in *Breathless* (Godard, 1960) the opening scene lacks an establishing shot and a conversation scene breaks the 180-degree rule.

German Expressionism

An influential German art movement of the 1910s and 1920s. German expressionist films have a highly stylised, distorted, anti-realist visual style.

Ideological critical approaches

Analysing a film critically from a particular ideological perspective to reveal dominant ideologies in a film or offer a more critical understanding of the film, e.g. a feminist reading of a film.

Ideology

Ideas, beliefs and values held by a person or groups in society. Political systems and parties are based around a system of ideas and principles, e.g. liberalism, socialism, etc.

Indiewood

The merging of Hollywood mainstream films and the American independent sector. It often refers to the subsidiaries of major studios who may produce and/or distribute independent-style films, e.g. Fox Searchlight and Sony Pictures Classics.

Intertextuality

When a film makes reference to another media text. The meaning may be shaped by the reference to another text, or a filmmaker may be paying homage to another film or media text.

Juxtaposition

The positioning of two shots, characters or scenes in sequence to encourage the audience to compare and contrast them.

Kammerspielfilm

A German film movement of the 1920s, characterised by a simple set design and a focus on character psychology. The films were often intimate domestic dramas about the lower-middle classes.

Knowledge organiser

A document, usually one or two sides of A4, containing key information and knowledge about a topic; useful for displaying knowledge in a systematic way.

Magic realism

Magic elements are added into a realistic depiction of the world. The magic elements are presented as normal and realistic. It can be used by filmmakers to portray an alternative reality and question the accepted reality.

Marxism

A left-wing ideology based on the 19th-century works of Karl Marx and Friedrich Engels. Marxists view capitalism as an economic and political system that creates class struggle, whereby the ruling class dominates and oppresses the working classes.

Montage

A film editing technique. In Russian montage films of the 1920s, montage was a theory and practice whereby meanings are created through the juxtaposition of shots edited together. In Hollywood cinema, montage commonly refers to a series of shots edited together to condense time, often with a musical track.

Narration

A commentary delivered to accompany a scene.

Narrative devices

Techniques used in order to tell a story.

New Hollywood

A period and movement in Hollywood cinema after the break-up of the studio era, from the late 1960s to the late 1970s. New Hollywood ushered in an auteur cinema, of new, young filmmakers who were influenced by European art-house movements. Characteristics of New Hollywood include morally ambiguous characters, innovative visual style and a re-working of classic Hollywood genres. New Hollywood is sometimes referred to as the American New Wave and the Hollywood Renaissance.

New wave

A new wave refers to a new movement or style of filmmaking which can often rejuvenate a national cinema with new and fresh ideas. New waves may develop due a wide range of factors, including changes in technology, a burgeoning of younger filmmakers, and responses to social, cultural and political factors. Examples include French New Wave (1958-1963) and Czech New Wave (1962-1968).

Postmodernism

A broad late-20th-century artistic and critical movement that departs from modernist ideas of objectivity, originality and single truths. Postmodern cinema is characterised by fragmentation, playfulness, heavy stylisation, intertextuality, a blurring of high and low culture and genre hybridity.

Realism

Film realism is a style which aims to create the effect of reality. Influential film critics such as André Bazin championed certain filmic techniques, including deep focus and long takes, as realistic devices which mimic the eye. There are many types of realism including social realism and classical realism.

Representations

How particular groups, people and places are depicted. In film studies, we consider how a representation is presented through elements of film form. The specification stipulates a focus on representations of age, ethnicity and gender.

Self-reflexive cinema

A film style that makes the audience aware of the process of filmmaking. It makes you aware of the film's own construction and artificiality.

Spectatorship

Spectatorship refers to the act of watching a film. Spectatorship explores how films address the individual spectator through the construction of the film and how the spectator is positioned. For example, one of the most common spectator positions in cinema is through the eyes of a male protagonist.

Structuralism

The idea that films can best be understood through an examination of their underlying structure, including exploring how meaning is produced through binary oppositions.

Studio system

A business model prevalent from 1927 to 1948 that ensured the dominance of a small number of major Hollywood studios. The Big Five Hollywood studios (20th Century Fox, RKO, Paramount, Warner Brothers and MGM) had control over production, distribution and exhibition, while the Little Three (Columbia, Universal and United Artists) controlled production and exhibition.

Surrealism

An international 20th-century movement of artists, writers and philosophers who valued the unconscious mind and dreams. They rejected conventional moral and artistic values. The surrealists were heavily influenced by the work of Sigmund Freud, particularly his book *The Interpretation of Dreams* (1899), which argued that our dreams reveal our unconscious motivations or desires.

Venn diagram

A diagram that shows relationships between two different things. When creating a Venn diagram for film studies, it can be used to show areas of overlap and difference between different films, styles, filmmakers, movement, etc.

Vertical Integration

When a company controls the different stages of a product's process or construction. During the studio era, the Big Five Hollywood studios were vertically integrated, as they controlled production, distribution and exhibition.